THREADS
OF
TREASURE

Sara Barnes

THREADS
OF
TREASURE

HOW TO MAKE, MEND, AND
FIND MEANING THROUGH THREAD

SCHIFFER
CRAFT

4880 Lower Valley Road • Atglen, PA 19310

Cover and interior design by Ashley Millhouse
Type set in Futura/Caecillia LT Pro

ISBN: 978-0-7643-6761-8
Printed in China

Published by Schiffer Craft
An imprint of Schiffer Publishing, Ltd.
4880 Lower Valley Road
Atglen, PA 19310
Phone: (610) 593-1777; Fax: (610) 593-2002
Email: Info@schifferbooks.com
Web: www.schifferbooks.com

For our complete selection of fine books on this and related subjects, please visit our website at www.schifferbooks.com. You may also write for a free catalog.

Schiffer Publishing's titles are available at special discounts for bulk purchases for sales promotions or premiums. Special editions, including personalized covers, corporate imprints, and excerpts, can be created in large quantities for special needs. For more information, contact the publisher.

We are always looking for people to write books on new and related subjects. If you have an idea for a book, please contact us at proposals@schifferbooks.com.

To my family
(including my cats).

CONTENTS

Shannon Moser

ACKNOWLEDGMENTS

I want to thank Marcia Young for first approaching me about writing this book and working with me to come up with the initial concept. This has been a dream. Thank you to all the artists who spoke with me, at great length, about their work. I have learned so much from each of you and am grateful for your contributions.

I also want to give special thanks to my parents, who have always supported me in any and all creative endeavors. I wouldn't be where I am without your love and encouragement.

HOW TO USE THIS BOOK

Disconnecting from your devices and creating work with your hands is at the heart of this book.

Before you read the next paragraph, take your phone and put it in another room. For 30 minutes or an hour, the device can cease to exist. It will be okay, I promise. Disconnecting from your devices and creating work with your hands is at the heart of this book. What's also important, perhaps equally as important, is that you find a way to do so in a free-from-digital time, in a place where you won't be disturbed by nagging notifications, dinging texts, or the inclination to google every question that runs through your head.

I was a child of the 1980s and early '90s, and I grew up on the cusp of personal technology becoming ubiquitous in many households. Although I was lucky to have a computer and internet from a young age, my experience differs from today; America Online was a service that we dialed into, and we couldn't stay on too long because it was clogging our only phone line. There was a clear delineation of computer time and no computer time. When I wasn't nestled in the cushy chair in Dad's office, I was elsewhere—getting my feet wet in the creek behind the house or concocting theories about how a washing machine ended up in the middle of the woods near our home.

I can't imagine going back to that way of using a computer, but it taught me to get into the habit of logging off. Technology is a place to come back to, not an ocean where we're trying to stay afloat. What's in front of us is important. Being here and choosing to make something with your hands is important.

We're about to begin a process of art making and of feeling creatively inspired. Human behavior favors a frictionless path. If you make something easy to do, make it easy to access, you're a lot more likely to do it.

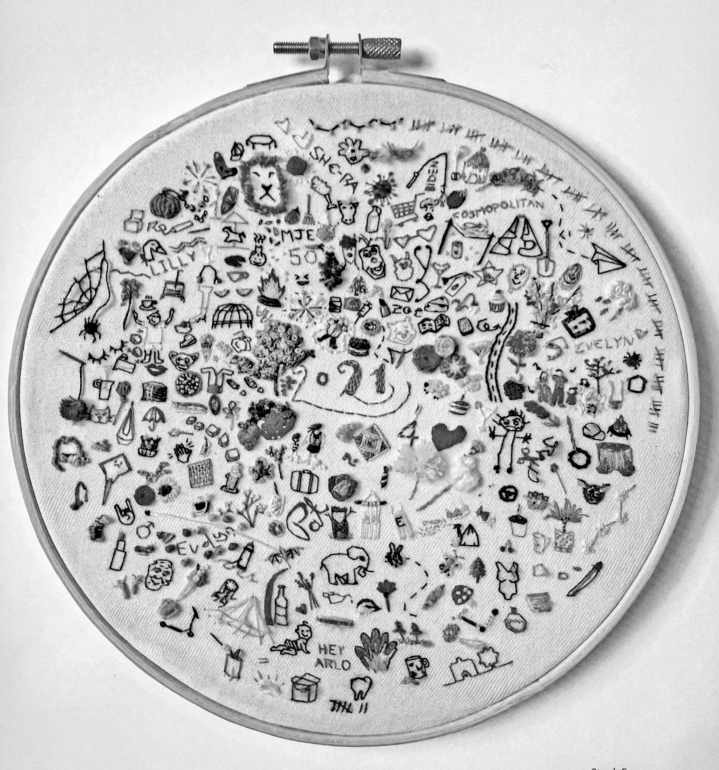

Steph Evans

We'll cover this later in the book, but if you truly want to treasure the experience ahead, you're going to want to put this book front and center wherever you create. By keeping this book next to your sewing machine or among your embroidery supplies, you're creating a path of least resistance to refer to the projects and artists featured in *Threads of Treasure.*

Just as essential as it is to make time for creativity, your attitude toward it is equally as important. Refrain from putting too many expectations on what you stitch, paint, or draw. It's challenging, especially today, to feel like you can do things just for fun. You know—the cornerstone of a hobby. Society has put a premium on production for the sake of others. It says, "What's the point of doing something if you can't monetize it?" But not everything you make has to be created as something to be sold to others. Try prioritizing your enjoyment and learning above getting a great photo or video to share on social media.

This book will help you cultivate your creativity through the lens of treasure. The artists here each encapsulate the notion of treasure in their work and use thread to do so.

In one section, you'll meet artists who incorporate found, foraged, or recycled objects into their work as a way to honor the natural world and the things that we consume. They view otherwise ordinary items and things that others see as trash as precious jewels with untapped potential.

Another portion of this book is dedicated to cherishing

It's challenging to feel like you can do things just for fun.

the things we already love, specifically in terms of clothing. It features artists who are dedicated to mending and/or adorning something instead of throwing it out. This practice multiplies treasure. What's old becomes new again, and in doing so the artist is making the statement that they treasure our environment.

The final part of this book focuses on treasuring the process of making by creating a consistent art practice consisting of daily projects. I speak with artists who dedicated days, months, and even years to one artistic endeavor as a way to commit to their creativity and treasure the process.

Each artist has something special to share about their life and work. Learning the inner workings of an artist—their background, how they generate ideas, etc.—is invaluable to art enthusiasts and professionals alike. Look closely and you're sure to find something that resonates with you. At the end of each section, you'll have the opportunity to put those concepts into practice and make something, too. We'll go through it together, as I will guide you with helpful prompts and techniques to try.

Meet artists who dedicate days, months, even years to one artistic endeavor as a way to commit to their creativity and treasure the process.

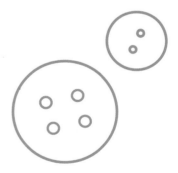

BEFORE YOU START

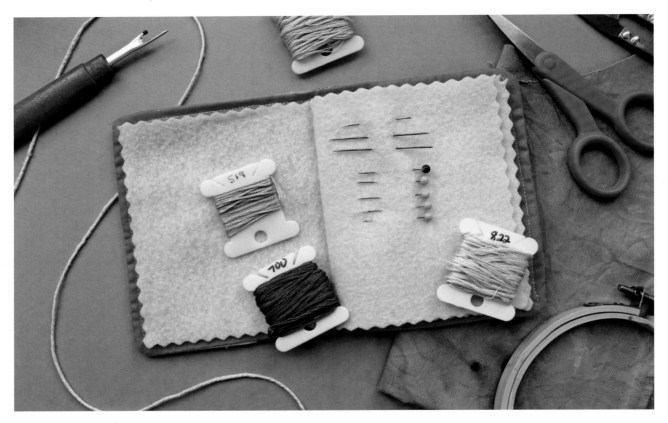

Some of the supplies you might use: a seam ripper, floss, needles, pins, fabric, scissors, and an embroidery hoop

Listen to your tools.
What do they tell you?

Supplies

There are basic supplies that you'll want to have on hand while you work. You might not need them all at once, but when the time comes, you'll be happy that you do have them. This list, it should be noted, is not an exhaustive one. But it's a place to start and perhaps a place to come back to if you're feeling stuck. Sometimes, a new tool can inspire a new way of working; the right embroidery hoop, for instance, can encourage you to work bigger. A fabric scrap collection encourages appliqué techniques. Be open to expanding upon your favorite tools, and listen to them, too. What do they tell you?

Needles

The world of needles is bigger than you might think. Some are made for embroidery, while others are ideal for mending clothes. For our purposes, we'll work mostly with embroidery needles (sometimes referred to as crewel needles). This style has a thinner shaft and sharp tip, perfect for piercing through fabrics. Embroidery needles come in various sizes; the smaller the number, the larger the needle in length and thickness. A size 5 needle is popular for beginner-level stitchers; however, many needles are sold in variety packs that range from sizes 3 to 9. Having a range of sizes is a great way to get a feel for the differences and to experiment with what works best for you.

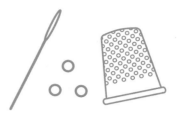

Crewel needles will work for some mending. If you're using thread or embroidery floss, the size of the needle eye isn't too important, since most thread should be able to go through it. But if you're using yarn, which is typically thicker than floss or even perle cotton, you'll want to use a darning needle. A darning needle is thick with a large eye. It has a blunt point and is ideal for making repairs in which holes are a visible part of the design.

Thread/Yarn

Selecting embroidery thread, a.k.a. floss, is one of my favorite parts of starting any stitching project. Floss makers offer so many colors—some as many as 400—that you can't help but want all of them. Luckily, floss is inexpensive and easy to find at your local craft store.

Basic floss skeins are typically made of cotton and contain six strands of thread that are spun together. The strands are loosely packed, meaning you can easily separate them based on your preference. I rarely, if ever, stitch with all six strands in my needle; doing so creates a thick line of thread and I find it harder to achieve the fine details I'm after in my embroidery. Some might balk at the use of just two strands (go ahead!) but it offers a lot of control. The downside is that it takes longer to cover an area of stitching because you're not covering as much surface area with each stitch made.

Cotton floss is the most popular type of embroidery thread, but it's not the only choice at the craft store. To add some pizzazz—and visual interest—to your work,

To add some pizzazz to your work, try incorporating other types of thread. Satin? Metallic? . . .

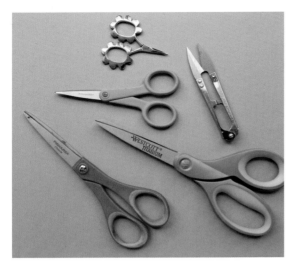

try incorporating other types of thread. Both satin and metallic flosses have a sheen to them that will be sure to catch your eye. Perle cotton is another favorite among crafters. It is a two-ply twisted thread that is nondivisible, meaning you can't separate the thread. Weightwise, its strands can be thicker than floss but thinner than yarn; like needles, it's available in a variety of sizes, and the smaller the numbers, the thicker the thread.

Scissors

It's always good to have more than one pair of scissors. Opt for a small pair that can trim threads and a big pair for fabric or other larger materials. To extend the life of your scissors, make them material specific. Don't commit the ultimate craft faux pas of using a pair to cut both fabric and paper; keep the fabric scissors for textiles only.

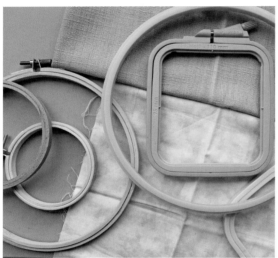

Embroidery Hoop

Embroidery hoops comprise two separate rings that are held together by a tightening screw. They are sold in a variety of sizes, the most popular materials being bamboo or plastic. Give both a try to discover your preference.

Not all hoops are round. Plastic hoops offer rectangle and square sizes, which are handy for certain designs.

Fabric

Where do I start with fabric? The possibilities are endless. You might've already started your fabric stash, or you're looking to kick off your collection. In general, opt for natural fibers over synthetic ones: cotton and linen or a linen blend. These will be easier to work with and are typically more amenable to dyeing or painting. Synthetic fabrics aren't off-limits, but use caution because they can be unpredictable. Avoid stretchy fabrics, since they can warp when you stitch.

In the spirit of sustainability, remember that thrift stores can offer a lot of fabric at affordable prices while giving the textile item a renewed life. Look for tablecloths, bedding, and even garments for the raw materials for your latest project. You're likely to find a lot of fabric and some interesting—maybe even vintage—surface design.

Sketchbook

Perhaps you thrive on spontaneity. You relish a random invite from a friend to grab a cup of coffee. Similarly, you approach a blank page or hoop with the same sort of enthusiasm. But if you're a planner—whether it's through writing, drawing, or a combination of the two—a sketchbook is sure to be a beloved part of your artistic practice. Get a small hardcover sketchbook to record your thoughts on the go, or opt for something bigger and fill it with preliminary sketches and notes.

When used regularly, a sketchbook can be a powerful tool. You can use it to mine for inspiration if you're feeling stuck and as a place to come back to when inspiration strikes. Or, use it as a place to record your artistic experiments: a dyeing recipe with great results or a color palette you'd like to use again.

As a tool, a sketchbook can be powerful for holding and finding inspiration.

Awl

An awl is a pointed tool with a handle that's used for piercing holes. It has a very sharp point and is commonly used in leatherworking, but its application can be in other materials too. The awl works well for stitching on paper and other rigid materials when you need to make a hole but the medium isn't pliable enough for a needle.

Glue

If you're not going to stitch it, chances are you're going to glue it. Just like it's good to have multiple pairs of scissors, you'll want a couple of different types of glue. A hot-glue gun is convenient tool, since it works on a variety of materials and cools quickly to create a strong bond. But glue guns have their downsides. The glue is thick and has to be spread with a nozzle, and you have less control over what you're gluing. It won't get into any fine crevices, and you can't spread it around. This can be a problem for large surface areas, especially if you're working with a rigid material. You'll have a lot of trouble gluing down the whole surface all at once.

This is why you should have some Tacky Glue in your craft stash. It is an all-purpose glue that adheres to many materials and dries with a clear and permanent bond. You can apply it using the nozzle on the bottle or with a brush and then wait 24 hours for it to be fully set.

Embellishments

In addition to your objects of treasure, think about embellishments to enhance your work. Some possibilities include beading, wires, or paper. If you can attach it with sewing or glue, it's an embellishment.

Seam Ripper

No one likes to make a mistake, but it's inevitable when you're sewing. A seam ripper is a handheld tool used for cutting and removing stitches. Its most common form has a handle, shaft, and forked head. To remove a stitch, slide the bottom of the head under the thread (or threads) that you want to remove.

Essential Stitching Techniques

The world of fiber art is vast, and there are so many different techniques to learn. But for the purposes of this book, here are some of the essential stitches you'll want to know before you begin.

Running Stitch

The running stitch, also called the straight stitch, is perhaps the most basic stitch of the more than 300 varieties in the world today. It consists of small, even lines that run on the front and backside of a cloth. They will never overlap. The nice thing about the running stitch is that it's great for temporarily holding something together. You'd use this stitch to baste a hem, for instance, before you finish it on your sewing machine.

To begin, pull your needle up through the back of your fabric until you reach the knot at the end of your thread. Then, pick a distance on the textile and bring the needle through to the backside. You'll be on the side where you started. Repeat this step by moving your needle to the same length that you made that last stitch.

That's it; the basic motion is up through the fabric and down the backside. Try to make each stitch a uniform length for consistency.

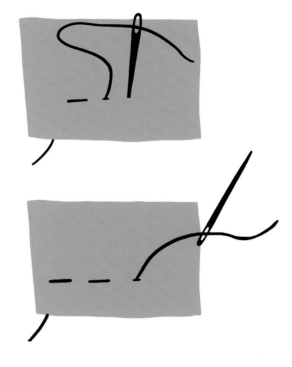

Satin Stitch

The satin stitch is a great fill stitch for both large and small areas. Start the technique by bringing the needle from the backside of your fabric to the front of it, pulling the knot until it's drawn tight. Then, insert the needle at a point opposite your original entry and pull it through to the backside.

On the back of the fabric, pick a point that's opposite to where you just pulled your needle through. You do not want the stitch to go in the same hole. Then, bring the needle up the backside and to the front of the fabric. You'll repeat these steps until you've filled the area with stitches. Make sure your stitches are touching each other, but not on top of one another. You will want them to lay flat and even, like the sheen of satin fabric.

This is a basic stitch, but you can make it look fancier by angling your stitches in different directions to create contrast. A chevron pattern is something easy to try and will give your satin stitch more flair. Just make sure your stitches remain opposite one another so that they never double back in the same hole.

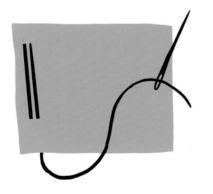

Blanket Stitch

A blanket stitch is an easy stitch to learn and sew. Aside from its ease, the stitch has a nice decorative element to it while also being secure. It's the best of both worlds.

The blanket stitch binds two pieces of fabric. Begin by holding the two slices of fabric in your hand, making sure the edges are separated. One will be your top piece and the other your bottom. Then, insert your threaded needle, maybe ¼ inch in, between the two pieces into the top fabric. Pull through the top piece. (The thread knot is in the center, now hidden.)

Now, go through both layers with your needle. Do this by taking the needle and bringing it to the bottom piece of fabric—the one that doesn't have any knots—and bringing it through the first hole that you made in the top fabric. You'll be in the same spot as when you started the stitch, but make sure you don't pull your thread tight through the hole. Leave a little slack; you should have a loop of thread.

The last step in making a blanket stitch is to guide your needle, approaching from the backward direction, through that loop, and pull it taut. This will secure the knot.

Replicate the blanket stitch by moving over a stitch width and taking your needle through the back of the fabric pieces. Again, leave some slack in the thread by not pulling the string all the way through your new hole. You'll have another loop of thread on the edge of your fabric. Take your needle and draw it through the loop and pull it tight. There will now be a "U"-shaped thread that binds the two fabrics together.

Repeat the step of bringing the needle through the backside of the fabric, making a loop, and then inserting the thread into the hole and pulling it closed.

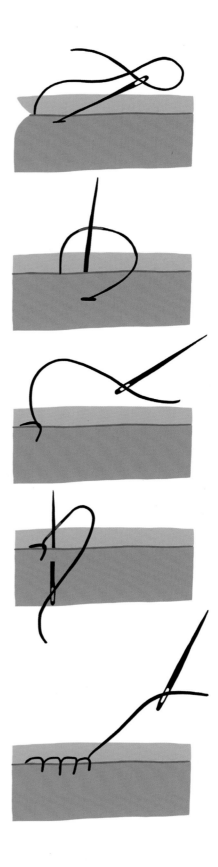

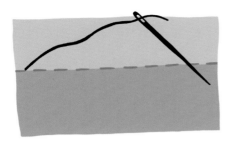

Whip Stitch

The whip stitch is similar to the blanket stitch in that it joins two pieces of fabric together. It has a similar look to the blanket stitch because of it, but the whip stitch can be less conspicuous if you make the stitches small.

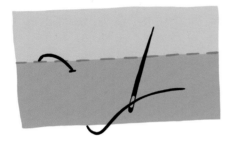

Begin this technique by loading your needle with knotted thread and starting in between your pieces of fabric. (This will conceal your knot.) Then, bring your needle through one of the pieces of the textile. If you're using this on appliqué, this would be the top of your design. With the needle now on one piece of your fabric, take the needle and bind the two pieces together. Do this by bringing your needle over the edge of the fabric and then poking it under where the thread came up. Then, angle your needle through both pieces of the textile, making sure that your thread will come up a short distance away from the stitch you just made.

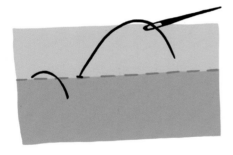

Continue going in and out until you've reached the end. After your last stitch, insert the needle through the backside and go through only one layer of the fabric. If you're working on appliqué, this would be the bottom layer. Once you reach the center of this textile sandwich, make a loop around the inner seam and create a small knot. Cut your thread and you're done.

Back Stitch

The back stitch is just that—a stitch that you work backward. (Aren't stitch names helpful?) Start by bringing your needle up through your fabric and then go one stitch length forward, bringing it through your fabric on the backside.

At this point, while on the backside, take your needle one stitch length forward and bring it up through the fabric again. You will have a stitch-length-sized space between your first stitch and the new one you just made.

Your needle and thread should be on the top side of the fabric now. Take that stitch backward to meet the point where your first stitch ended, and insert the needle in the hole. Then, repeat the process.

For smaller, curved outlines, it's best to make your stitches very small to create a smooth edge. If your stitches are too wide, the outlined shape will look angular and even a bit jagged.

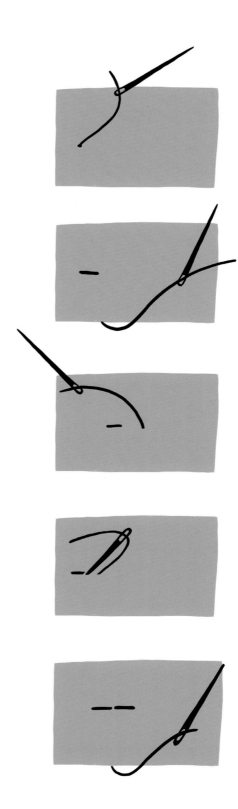

Get into the Making Mindset

Having the right tools and knowing some basic techniques is important. But what is also vital is approaching your artistic practice with the right mindset. Our perceptions of the world around us are filtered through mindsets that influence our lives in quietly profound ways.

Alia Crum, a psychologist who researches the power of mindsets, shares what she has learned about the topic. "So often we think that our beliefs, our experiences, are a direct reflection of the world as it objectively is," she says, "[but] our perceptions, our beliefs, our experience are always an interpretation. They're always filtered through the lenses, the mindsets, that we have."[1]

A mindset is a belief, and the views we hold can help us achieve great things. Believing that something is possible shapes how we interact with the world and respond to the challenges that come along with it.

This is particularly helpful when it comes to learning something new. Chances are you're going to struggle some when acquiring a skill set. But if you're of the mindset that learning takes time and that you just have to keep going—eventually you'll get it—you're likely to stick with it when the going gets tough.

Before you begin to read the stories of artists and immerse yourself into the projects in this book, get into a making mindset.

A making mindset is a nonjudgmental one. It looks at craft problems as solvable.

View the act of reading and working with your hands as important tasks that make you feel human. Doing so grounds you, and you deserve to be able to have this time to reconnect with yourself. Pat yourself on the back!

Because you're making time for this, let yourself play and try to avoid placing too many value judgments on what you create. You showed up, and that's the important part. Recognize that you might not know a technique for something and you'll have to learn. It might be tough to master, but it will never be that hard again. (It might be challenging in different ways, but never in that same way.)

A making mindset is a nonjudgmental one. It looks at craft problems as solvable.

So, you're here. Get ready to learn and observe—not only what the other artists in this book have created, but what you feel a connection to or curiosity about. What about it is so interesting? This is when you'll want to pore over the details and closely analyze what you're doing. When you can pinpoint what it is about something that resonates with you, you can bring an element of that into your work, both present and future.

This can appear in small and unexpected ways. During an art history class in college, for instance, I remember a slide lecture in which the professor was showing images of mosaic art from the Byzantine Empire. The artworks depicted people with some suggestion of form, but the overall aesthetic was stylized and fairly flat—something that I already identified as something I loved. But in this instance, I noticed the style of the eyes. They were exaggerated almonds and were pleasing to my own eyes. This momentary observation changed the way I've drawn eyes ever since, and it has continued to encourage me to approach things with openness.

As you make these observations, remember them—whether it's stored in your head or in a notebook. Little by little, you'll collect them and figure out how all of these pieces fit together and develop your artistic voice.

But, back to right now. Whether you're reading or making (or both), keep in mind that you're treasuring something you love. You are honoring your time as well as the objects you choose to display, make, or mend. It's something to celebrate. You are a maker!

You are honoring your time as well as the objects you choose to display, make, or mend. It's something to celebrate.

CHAPTER ONE

DISPLAYING TREASURES

When we have something we want to remember, it's often commemorated in a photograph. A picture is easy to frame and to cherish when it's sitting on a desk or a bookshelf, but what about the other objects we collect? Or, what if the items don't represent a memory, but something else that's important to you? They're not as easy or as intuitive to display as a picture frame.

This section of the book is focused on showcasing treasures by way of fiber art. Treasures can mean many things. In the scope of this book, they are referring to any object that has meaning to you. It could be as innocuous as a bottle cap or as fancy as a jewel. We apply our own values to things.

Contemporary fiber artists are creating beautiful work that is informed by the things they've found and shaped by their lens of the world. I've spoken to Hilary Waters Fayle, Janis Ledwell-Hunt, Clarissa Callesen, Jessica Grady, and Shannon Moser about their work, and our conversations cover the expected topics of what their art looks like and how they create it.

But beyond any formal aspects, I'm interested in what led them to art making and how past experiences have shaped what they are creating today. Genuine artistic expression is the culmination of years of producing things while also being introspective and considering how everyday life can inform someone's creative voice.

There's something to learn from each of these artists, and the "You Can Do It" portion of the chapters invites you to find a small object and build art around it. Incorporating something that you already love provides a starting point that is uniquely you but connects you to the same wonderful world of makers throughout the world and history.

This can sound intimidating; you're essentially being asked to create something from scratch. But fear not. I will take you through some brainstorming techniques about your object, and then explain why creating a series of rough sketches (called thumbnails) will help you think through multiple ideas.

Before you grab a needle and thread, you'll have a plan of what you're going to create while leaving open the possibility for experimentation and spontaneity. And if you're feeling really stuck—don't worry, I've been there—I'll show you exactly how I approached it. You can follow along with me or take some of the advice from the artists and work it into what you will do.

Hillary Waters Fayle

Leaves are an unconventional canvas for embroidery. They are known for being brittle; if you've ever delighted in hearing the crunch of leaves under your boots in October, you'll know what I'm talking about. But any preconceived notions about their lacking sturdiness are challenged when you see the work of Hillary Waters Fayle. Hillary fuses embroidery with nature by stitching designs onto leaves of various shapes and sizes.

"I'm most drawn to patterns—natural pattern, but also geometric pattern," she tells me. "Patterns found in sacred geometry and the way that those relate to natural patterns is really, really interesting to me. I also look at a lot of historical textiles, and traditional textile references." Beyond textiles, Hillary looks to botany and botanical art for inspiration.

So often in life, things are cyclical. If you look back on decades past, there are bound to be things that you liked as a kid that still resonate with you, in some way, in your life today. It's hard to see that pattern when you're in it, but upon reflection, it's comforting to know that as much as things change, constants remain. Tapping into this can also forge new and exciting paths in your work.

Hillary spent a lot of her childhood exploring the outdoors in upstate New York, outside Buffalo. She traipsed through the nearby woods and her family's garden. She made forts and tried to decipher bird calls.

At the same time, Hillary felt compelled to make things. The young creative enjoyed drawing and painting, sure, but crafting things was important to her. "I wanted things that I was going to use," she recalls, "and I wanted to whittle. My parents were like, 'We're not giving you a knife.' And so I kind of found my way to the needle and thread because they're so accessible."

The two interests in Hillary's orbit never connected. But as she got older, they were getting closer. "When I was 14," she explains, "I went to summer camp that was pivotal in my life. It was based around this idea of teaching kids about the environment and about how to be better stewards of the land and how to protect what we have, and just think a little bit differently about it."

The camp was a defining moment for Hillary. "It was the first time I kind of realized, oh, something that's really worthy of my time in my life is to devote myself to figuring out how to protect what I care about, which is nature and the environment." She later volunteered at the camp until she was 18.

Hillary went to college and focused her studies on fiber art and textiles. During her junior year, she studied abroad in Manchester, England. "[I] went to England and they have a specific degree in embroidery," she explains. "I just thought it was the most incredible thing, and I fell really deep into learning about the history of needlework and just the different ways that cultures use needlework for storytelling and for decorating important textiles, for religion, for ritual, for historical reasons. You could fall deep into that hole and never see the bottom."

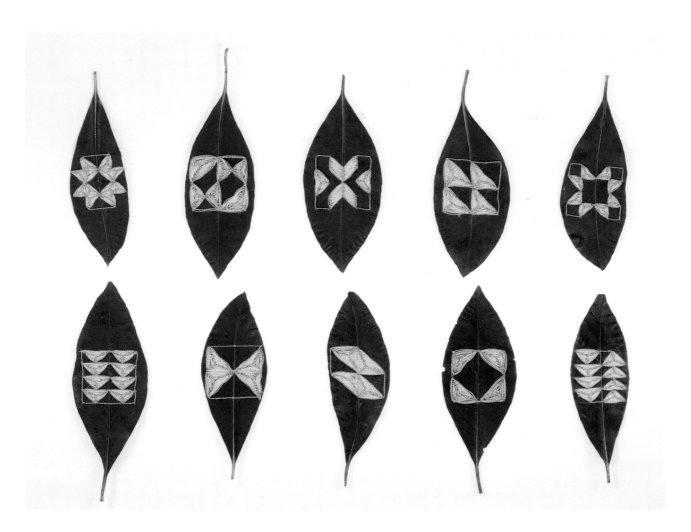

Hillary was enthralled by embroidery, and while there she became interested in joining (or insertion) stitches—a variety of stitches that attach two pieces of fabric—which serve both a decorative and functional purpose. At the same time, she was working on a small scale; she was across the pond, after all, and everything needed to fit in her suitcase when she went home.

Summer came, and Hillary got a paid job at the same camp that had made such an impact on her as a kid. She continued to work there until she was 26 years old and while she went to grad school. Her job was as a camp cook, and she had a lot of free time between preparing meals. The downtime yielded valuable hours full of potential artist materials—and Hillary knew where to look.

Her interest in fiber art and nature, the joining stitches she pored over in England—it all came full circle.

"Leaves are a lot stronger than they seem."

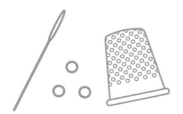

All these years later, Hillary remembers sitting under an oak tree and having a hunch that she could stitch on one of its leaves. She was right, and this feeling of sublime washed over her. Her interest in fiber art and nature, the joining stitches she pored over in England—it all came full circle.

"I was thinking about those insertion stitches and the literal joining of two things together," she recalls. "It was Aha!, I can not only physically join the leaves together with the stitching, but it's also a way to conceptually bind these two things that I care about, and feel this connection with."

Hillary is quick to say that she doesn't own the idea of stitching on leaves, and those who want to try it should go ahead. But it will take years of work, of experimentation, to get to a place where you marry consistency with the amount of desired detail.

"Leaves are a lot stronger than they seem," Hillary declares. "They're seemingly so delicate, and they are delicate. But it's this symbol of delicacy and fragility that I think really works for what I'm kind of talking about, which is that when we're gentle and we're thoughtful about the way we're doing something, it's a metaphor for what's possible."

Hillary stitches onto leaves she describes as "thick" and "sturdy." These particular characteristics vary depending on location. She now lives in Richmond, Virginia, an area that offers a plethora of trees that stay green year-round. If a type of leaf is meant to stick around through the colder seasons, it will likely be hardy and waxy—an ideal combination for embroidery.

Creating artwork atop leaves requires gathering them, whether that's picking a few off a trail during your hike or finding the perfect one on a tree branch. For guidance on the ethical concerns of taking from the land, Hillary has referred to the book *Braiding Sweetgrass: Indigenous Wisdom, Scientific Knowledge and the Teachings of Plants* by Robin Wall Kimmerer. The author is a member of the Citizen Potawatomi Nation and a scientist interested in the restoration of ecological communities and restoring our relationship to the land.

Hillary abides by the rules of never taking more than she needs and never taking more than half.

In *Braiding Sweetgrass*, Kimmerer shares the Honorable Harvest, which is an "Indigenous canon of principles and practices that govern the exchange of life for life."[1] To find leaves for her work, Hillary abides by the rules of never taking more than she needs and never taking more than half.

"I always think about and ask the question 'Should I take this?'" Hillary shares. "And then [I] listen to the answer. There's a respectful way of working with natural materials and working with things that are growing, and I always try to be careful about that."

A good rule of thumb when selecting what you're going to work with is to consider if you find it interesting. It sounds like a no-brainer, but it's easy to forget. We tend to underestimate how long a particular work of art will take. If you're not feeling passionate about your material, getting through that middle-of-a-project slog will be a challenge.

Hillary looks for leaves that are "curious in some way." And they don't have to be perfect, either. She'll pick up leaves that have insect bites, strange coloration, or some sort of disease that makes them look abnormal.

With her found or fallen leaves gathered, Hillary uses a very small needle to embroider her designs. She is careful in the way she holds the leaves as she works, and makes sure to support them with each stitch. The space between stitches is another factor. Leaves, similar to other materials such as paper, aren't as forgiving as fabric because they don't stretch. Having the stitch holes too close together creates one bigger hole and can ruin what you're working on.

Once her work is complete, Hillary avoids reinforcing the leaves if at all possible. "For me, so much about what this is, is wonder. There's wonder and magic in it. And it's more exciting to me to work just with the leaf itself and not have it reinforced in any way. Because I know if I reinforce it, it's gonna be fine. If I don't do that, it's more of an achievement. It's more exciting. It's more remarkable to me."

Janis Ledwell-Hunt

Janis Ledwell-Hunt has a dead box. It sounds haunting, but the container plays an important role in her creative process. It often signals the beginning of her sculptures. As she waits for the animals in it to decay, she'll eventually combine the skulls with macrame-made mushrooms, leaves, coral, and more. In doing so, she breathes new life into these deceased creatures.

When I speak with Janis, a college professor turned artist, in the background is a window with tall trees leading into a forest. She lives in the Comox Valley in British Columbia, Canada, "just around the corner from the ocean." Janis has dogs who have a knack for finding things that have naturally died. For anyone who lives in an area surrounded by dense nature, this probably comes as no shock. (For city dwellers, maybe you've been caught off guard.)

Janis finds beauty in the bones. My initial response is to attach sadness to them, since these creatures are no longer alive. But Janis has a different way of looking at her discoveries. "It makes me feel more comfortable with the notion of death," she explains. "To have somebody find you in that kind of state and find . . . value in your decapitation. There's something that's so much nicer about that. In Western human civilizations, let's say, we often want to hide that away, and we want to make bodies look like they're strangely alive in a coffin."

The skull series is an opportunity to create an alternative narrative for the bones—to imagine an outcome of them by way of art. One of Janis's most striking pieces features an animal skull with the top of the head removed. In that empty space are her colorful macrame creations. They offer a stark contrast to the rigidity of the bones, from the greens and pinks to the gentle fuzziness of the yarn.

"It makes me feel more comfortable with the notion of death," she explains.

Discovering a skull in this condition was unusual. "When you find a skull," Janis explains, "it's not in this pristine form. I found it with the head sawed off, and that created this perfect opening."

Then came the obvious question. What goes in its place? "I was thinking about adding mushrooms and ferns and leaves and flowers." In doing this, she fills an absence. A void. They're no longer vacant skulls. "[I] punctuate the absences of the parts of the skeleton that had been removed or worn away over time."

Over the course of our conversation, Janis reconsiders the poignancy of the skulls. "If there's a sadness in it," she contemplates, "it's taking it out of that environment where I found it, right? So part of the mourning, the lamentation, that might be there is 'What might have grown out of this had it been left behind?' I take it because I just assumed somebody else will take it if I don't. But what would it look like if that were to remain in that space and become overgrown?"

Janis has a unique perspective in pondering this idea. She was a tree planter for 12 years and spent her summers and springs (and sometimes falls) traversing rough logging roads. She and her fellow crew members would arrive at the worksite, referred to as the cut block, and plant hundreds of young saplings.

"We came to think about a cut block as this scar of industry," Janis says. "Where you're cutting down trees and removing an animal's habitat." It's destructive, and it can be hard to see past that. Janis and her partner returned to the cut blocks years later and witnessed nature's resilience. "Yes, some trees were growing," she recalls, "but interestingly, there were also spaces where we'd go pick berries." Snakes emerged from the shadows, and animals were drawn to the new growth.

"I'm really invested in the way in which something of value, or something regenerative, comes from active, even industrial destruction. You've got to find some form of meaning in them, I suppose," she remarks. "For me, it's more about the fantasy of 'What would this look like if I were able to happen upon it years from now?'"

Filling the skulls requires careful arrangements, not unlike when a florist plucks and places all the flowers and

> "What is it that you have and that you can be influenced by in your immediate environment?"

greenery so that when done, the whole thing sings. Janis will separately make macrame mushrooms, a series of individual leaves, twisted vines, and any other element she wants to include. She does nearly all of it with recycled or upcycled materials. Noting that her supplies are "imperfect" since she's not making her own fibers, Janis sources and uses materials that are recycled and would otherwise end up in a landfill.

Once she has everything created, she spends a lot of time trying to place each item into its skull or on a piece of driftwood. "What [I'm looking for] is where I have absences and gaps that I can punctuate with something else, with some sort of form of emergent life." This is painstaking and slow work. If you've ever tried to arrange flowers or style a bookshelf, you might know the feeling. You only know how the different items speak to one another once they're together. "I obsess over color and dimension and size," Janis explains, "and really trying to think of what will pop in certain places or what palette works really well together."

Janis believes that we all have something unique to say through our art—even if we don't think we do. From art enthusiasts to professional artists, we are all plagued with the thought that what's said has already been spoken and what's created is already made. It's this sort of fatalistic thinking that will stop anyone in their tracks. What we often fail to remember is that everything we do is imbued with ourselves.

Janis uses an everyday conversation as an example. "[The way] you move through your life is pretty darn different [from someone else]. The person that's on the other end is going to have different tones, different inflections, different kinds of introspective moments . . ." You get the picture.

You just have to get used to tapping into this voice. For that, Janis has some tips. "Look around your space," she recommends. "What is it that you have and that you can be influenced by in your immediate environment?"

You don't have to have it all figured out at once. "[Don't beat] yourself up about trying to compose this completely original idea that no one else has ever thought about," Janis says. Instant won't work; "you won't arrive at anything that looks like [an authentic] voice." But keep working at it and you will.

Clarissa Callesen

Fecundity, 2016

Clarissa Callesen has had a winding path in her journey to fiber art. Just like her work is an alluring collection of colors, textures, and found objects, her seemingly disparate experiences are what inform her work today.

"I didn't really find creativity until I was in [community] college," she tells me from Bellingham, Washington. After arriving there for a theater scholarship, she became frustrated with the department, left, and found solace in the art department.

But when she transferred to art school, that wasn't a great fit either. Clarissa stayed for one quarter before dropping out and getting a tattoo apprenticeship. She tattooed for six years and learned a valuable lesson she still carries today. "You show up at this time to make art," she says, "whether you feel like it or you don't." By showing up, even if you're not feeling it that day, you're still moving the needle forward on what it is that you ultimately want to do. For Clarissa, this was to make a living as an artist.

After tattooing came an apprenticeship with pottery. Clarissa worked as a functional potter for many years, eventually becoming a part owner in a pottery gallery. All this time, she was still working on her own pieces and used what she learned from her jobs to inform where she went next—and ultimately to where she is today.

Clarissa has long been a collector of "weird junk and trash" and is fascinated by what found objects can signify. "I love the idea that you can pick up a piece of broken pottery off the beach, and it's trash, or it's how we see trash, but we don't know its story," she says. "And I love thinking about the fact that perhaps that teacup was somebody's grandmother's [that] she drank out of every

Fecundity (detail)

Fecundity (detail)

day for 10 years, and [it] broke on a specific day. I love the potential that there is to always have a deeper story to that which is completely mundane."

This love of an object's history—its innate story—motivated Clarissa to start working with assemblage during her time as a potter. She began crafting art dolls based on things she would find at the Goodwill Outlet, which is full of items that the thrift stores couldn't sell (its wares are available to purchase by the pound).

"I am really drawn to texture," she explains when I asked how, exactly, she knows what to pick up or to pass on. "So, things that show their age. Rusty stuff, crusty pieces of painting. Color isn't a big thing for me, because my color palette tends to be neutral."

"You show up at this time to make art," she says, "whether you feel like it or you don't."

"One of the things I love about fabric, which is the same as one of the things I loved about clay, is fabric can mimic so many different materials."

Spear, 2016

Spear (detail)

Tender Shelter (detail)

THREADS OF TREASURE

Clarissa's art dolls, while figurative and recognizable as dolls, were ultimately what led her to her current body of work. She began adding more cloth to their bodies, and the dolls became larger—so big that they were almost life size. That, coupled with studying the works of inspirational abstract artists, drew her to depicting the nonrepresentational by way of textiles and fibers.

"I have no formal fiber art training," Clarissa shares. "I can't even knit or crochet." But it didn't stop her. "I am a big believer of 'jump in when you don't know what you're doing.' Because from that, you find ways that are different, you find ways that are original, because you're not tying it into specific ideas about what medium is supposed to be."

Clarissa has found that when you immerse yourself in a subject, you'll learn what you don't know. By identifying your lack of knowledge, you'll be able to ask the right questions and find the resources to help you with the answer.

"I think that some of my uniqueness to my technique and the way I work is by combining different ways of working," she reflects. "One of the things I love about fabric, which is the same as one of the things I loved about clay, is fabric can mimic so many different materials."

Clarissa looks at her materials like a puzzle. "I'm not much of a sketcher. The way I work is [that] I'm inspired by my materials and inspired by moving things around. I like to think [I'm] assembling a puzzle where I don't know what the end picture is." She plays around with what is in front of her. How many different ways, for instance, she can put stuffing inside cloth or what would happen if she burned the ends? There's only one way to find out.

Not all of it is successful or the easiest way to do things. But the lessons learned and experience gained have taught Clarissa about letting go of the idea that there is a right or a wrong.

Arranging and assembling a piece reveals its concepts, which often examine the worth we place on items perceived as discard. "I'm really interested in how we look at what the value is in those brush piles, which are unsightly, [but] become this environment for birds and insects and compost and growth, and the production of food—the blackberries," she explains.

Tender Shelter, 2018

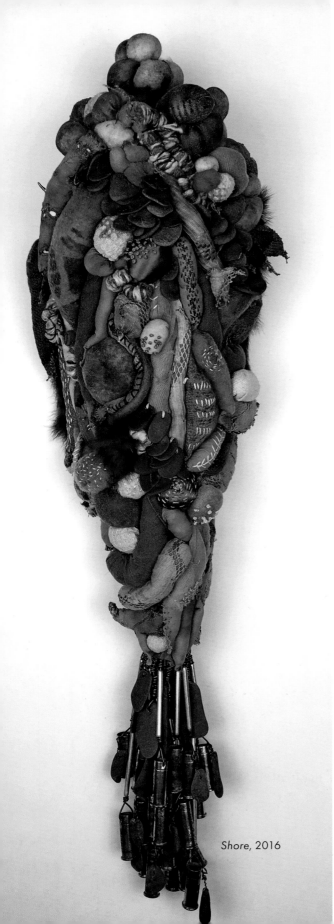

Shore, 2016

Taking that same concept, she compares it to a hairbrush she found on the road that had been run over many times by traffic. "It could've easily been trash, but it became a piece of artwork." Clarissa examines and challenges the things we're so quick to discard, and pauses long enough to see value in them. "The growth comes from those places."

From a technical standpoint, the fabric, hairbrushes, wood, and beyond are built on a metal armature. The individual elements are sewn or wired onto that. (She avoids using glue whenever possible.) Once things are laid out, she starts stitching the "clumps" together. "I go from having tiny puzzle pieces to larger puzzle pieces," Clarissa says, before everything comes together in one cohesive form.

Clarissa offers a tip for anyone who wants to start using found or foraged objects in their work. She challenges us to separate its identification from its form.

"Look at a found object as a form," she instructs. "What is its shape? What is its texture? What is its color? Try to separate that from its function. We see a piece of trash, and immediately our human nature—doesn't matter what we do—makes us want to go to identification. We're going to identify what it did, what it's supposed to do.

"I think that when we can look at something as shape and texture and shadow, that allows us to work with things in a different way." This will likely take some practice, and it might make us feel uncomfortable.

"We have a lot of pressure as artists, or even just in this culture, to go in one direction. We need to specialize or we need to have a specific style," she says. "I think that that can really stifle an artist. I know that I struggle with that. [But] when we trust ourselves, and we try different things, that's where we bring in ingenuity and originality."

Sound, 2016 (detail)

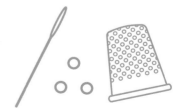

Shore (detail)

Jessica Grady

The plastic strip from a bubble mailer and the metallic insides of a chip bag can be treasures. If we look at them as the potential raw materials for art, they can be reborn as something spectacular—far beyond their humble beginnings. Jessica Grady composes her maximalist sculptural embroideries entirely out of recycled materials.

From beading to bottle caps, nearly everything that Jessica comes across can be used in her work. Her pieces are heavily layered with the unconventional materials that you can't help but want to touch. For her, increasing this sensory experience is keeping in line with her artwork's "more is more" philosophy.

Jessica's current body of work is informed by her background in textile design. "My specialties," she tells me, "were hand stitching, embellishments, and prints that focus on color, and [the] idea of intricate detail." She worked in the fashion industry after college and saw the environmental impacts of consumerism. It influenced how she approached her work, and she began recycling and repurposing materials to make her own embellishments.

Jessica views her use of recycled materials as a way to reduce her overall environmental impact while showing folks that making art is more accessible than we think. "Rather than telling people [that] they have to buy loads of expensive materials, they can really use what they already have, or what's going to be thrown in the bin."

Jessica's collection includes things you likely have on hand yourself, such as bubble mailers, the packaging from sweet treats, and shiny plastics that aren't recyclable. Beyond that, she will use paper remnants and anything she doesn't want to see go in the trash can. It's as

easy as being mindful of what you throw away, but Jessica will also seek out items that others are wanting to dispose of by visiting scrap stores.

"We have these things called scrap stores [in the UK]," she explains, "They're not like a thrift store, in the fact that it's all industrial waste. So you get things like the off-cuts from fabric, or different factories will send stuff to them that they would normally send to landfill." The special shop has "loads of weird things" that she wouldn't be able to buy anywhere else. "They have the neoprene circles that they get from a wetsuit factory. It's the area of the wetsuits where the head gets chopped out. I get all these stacks of neoprene circles from the wetsuit and I make sequins."

Just like an artist will have different paints for their palette, Jessica's materials vary in finish, texture, and color and are stored in recycled spice jars. She pairs their

Though they're immensely detailed and extremely considered, Jessica doesn't plan her compositions beforehand.

various characteristics to add visual variety to her embellished pieces. From afar, they are vibrating as one. But once you study them up close, you notice these intimate moments between the materials that are also happening throughout the composition. A painted disc, for instance, will act as a base that's topped with fluorescent-colored mesh stitched with yarn. Capping it is a tiny bead that's like a cherry on top. And that's just one small section of her overall piece.

By using the disparate elements in this way, Jessica transcends their original use and transforms them into something that's not only beautiful but is a compelling comment on consumption. And on how, in the right context, the ordinary is made one of a kind.

Though they're immensely detailed and extremely considered, Jessica doesn't plan her compositions beforehand. Rather, she allows the collected items to speak to her. "My work is quite inspired by the materials rather than looking [at] a flower or some sort of very specific idea," she shares. "For me, the ideas come through the materials and thinking of their potential, whether they can crinkle or whether they can be folded or pleated, and what they're gonna do in different ways, depending on what I'm working with, whether that's plastic or metal or paper or fabric."

It's about seeing what these materials are capable of. How do they act beyond their intended purpose? "It's the idea of embellishing embellishments. So, physically using something like a hard material, like a hard plastic, or a shell or something found, and actually stitching into that as a surface on its own, and then adding it in."

Regardless of the material, every part of Jessica's work is attached via hand stitching—no glue is necessary. It's why there is so much layering in her work; certain elements will stabilize the composition.

"I think of it as layering up," she explains. "So [with] each element that I add onto the layer, I embellish it first by adding stitch to it before I then stitch it on." Figuring out the perfect (for her) combination is like a jigsaw puzzle, especially because she's arranging without a solid plan. "It's very much letting the pieces evolve as I add each layer to them."

Jessica remains open to the possibility that things will change as she works, and they often do. "I might envisage something when I get started. And by the time I finished, it's completely different, because it's sort of taken its own little journey."

Although her plan is to not have a plan, that doesn't mean that Jessica works in a completely spontaneous way. Guidelines naturally reveal themselves depending on the scope of her project. Size is one factor that will determine the kind of items she's able to use in a piece. Jessica also considers scale. The more she layers pieces, the smaller the details become. "I normally add my hand embroidery," she says. "Little decorative stitches that I see as little tiny patterns, or little tiny details. They always are the last thing that I add. So if I'm putting them on, I know that it's finished."

By collecting your items of discard for a few days or a week, you too can transform them into one-of-a-kind works of art. Jessica recommends starting small. "I think papers are quite a nice thing to start off with, because ev-

Regardless of the material, every part of Jessica's work is attached via hand stitching.

erybody has envelopes that come in the post, or old magazines or catalogs."

The key is challenging yourself to see something in a different way. "Maybe consider how something could be used," Jessica offers. "Or it could be something as simple as using a broken necklace, or chopping up maybe an item of clothing that has a stain on it or something." You don't need new, just a creative eye. "Just using what is there, having that as the material rather than using brand-new beads or sequins or other things that you would normally put onto something."

When it's time to stitch your materials onto something, denim is Jessica's top pick. "Because it's a dark color, whatever you put on top is really gonna pop It gives you lots of flexibility for colors and for different materials." All of her embellishments are basic shapes, which is also something to keep in mind; the visual complexity of her work comes from the way the elements are arranged.

"Simple is key. It doesn't need to be a complex thing. Something like squares or circles, triangles, and taking something—whether that's a piece of paper, a piece of fabric—and chopping it up into little shapes. Then, just using a simple needle and thread to do a little straight stitch through each little piece and add it on to the base." Go on and build from there.

You can do this all without the use of glue. An embroidery stitch can become another design element and an easy way to create a pattern in addition to joining pieces. "If you stitch over [a stone] and have that line, you've got a little stripe," Jessica muses. "You could then think about color and think about maybe having two different threads."

There is no set path for this type of making, nor are there any rules. Creatively, it's freeing. And from a sustainability perspective, this way of thinking speaks to the larger actions we all need to take.

"Everybody has a part to play," she reminds us. "No matter how small. Even just reusing something that was destined to be thrown away is being quite innovative with your materials. It will give you more ideas than using something that's just bought, because you're actively encouraging yourself to think about things in a different way." Remember: "Even if it's a small thing, it all adds up."

Shannon Moser

You might be reading this section of the book and be quietly fretting that you don't have any treasure to incorporate into a work of art. That's okay and understandable; perhaps you're the "leave only footprints" type of person when you're out in nature, or nothing comes to mind when you imagine a treasure. You have a special memory, but it's in the form of a photograph.

If you don't have an object but would like to honor that memory, try taking a cue from Shannon Moser. Creating under the name Native Sage Threads, she works from her own photographs to create hoop art that's inspired by her road trips to the mountains and the desert—her two favorite landscapes.

Shannon starts by going through her photography and considering which images can translate to embroideries. Her work isn't limited to floss; she looks for materials that excite her, and manipulates them to fit her desired imagery. "I found wool yarn at a public market," she tells me in Seattle, "and I unraveled it a little bit to sluff it up." Doing this led to her forming fluffy clouds that are above red-rock embroideries and mountain scapes. Lace is an unlikely complement to desert sand, but it's paired with beads that evoke a sculptural element like cairns you'd see while hiking. There is harmony and rhythm to it all.

We don't often let ourselves play and create without expectation, but seeing where a technique will lead is how Shannon pushes forward in her work. "I had the idea to do [rock] towers with a variegated thread, and then I thought about how when the sun shines on these cliffs, there are certain parts where the rock really shines," she recalls. "I felt like I could really bring that out with highlighting with beads, and that's what made me try that."

Feeling a connection to the material is also important. Shannon is conscious of how something feels when she's using it. She's tried conventional acrylic painting (not with embroidery), but she didn't feel a relationship to it like she has to her "paint." When she feels a connection, like she does with embroidery and mixed media, she knows others will, too.

Her work isn't limited to floss; she looks for materials that excite her.

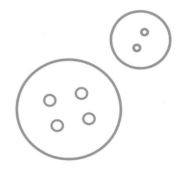

YOU CAN DO IT:

Create an Artwork Displaying a Treasure

Before you begin this project, you'll want to spend time finding your object of treasure. You might've thought of something right away, or you need a little time to think. Either way, give yourself the space and time that you need. But as you consider your object of treasure, here's what to keep in mind.

Type of Treasure

The type of treasure you choose to incorporate in your work is completely up to you. We apply our own value to the objects in our possession. While this is the case, consider the form of this item. Is it a flat object? What is its material? How would you adhere it to fabric or paper? Would you want to?

One item that I treasure is a small shell that I found on the shore of Washington State when I was at the beach with my parents during our annual beach trip. I enjoy walking on the beach with them and their golden retrievers, scouring for shells among the natural debris washed up by the shore. It's hard to find a shell at the particular beach we go to, but when you do it feels like a gift.

Selecting something with a story attached is a way to choose meaning for the object at hand. It's an important consideration, but also keep in mind whether an object or item of clothing will hold up to the stress of being handled as you incorporate it into a work or mend it. For example, the oils in our hands can degrade something we cherish, and very old cloth might fray beyond recovery.

Preparation

Let's go back to that shell I found. Using the bauble in a work of art is possible, but it takes special consideration. A shell is tough, but it's not indestructible. It'd be unwise to use it in a way where there is pressure applied to it, since it could break. There are a couple of options for it: gluing it, or stitching it in place with thread. Floss allows its integrity to remain intact, but it's more of a challenge to keep it sturdily attached in the piece. Gluing might be the best option to ensure that it stays put while the integrity remains intact. But, of course, gluing is permanent.

It's easy to see how you can perform mental gymnastics when working with unconventional materials or items in need of repair. You'll want to carefully consider what's best for your item at hand. Sometimes, the best way to honor something is to not put it in a situation in which it will be compromised or destroyed.

When working with an object, make sure that it's clean and that any broken bits have been removed or repaired.

A shell is tough, but it's not indestructible. It'd be unwise to use it in a way where there is pressure applied to it.

Once you've selected your item of treasure, it's now time to honor it through artwork. Great! Now comes one of the most challenging parts of the process: coming up with ideas of what your piece will look like. If your blood ran cold after reading that last sentence, fear not. I will take you through the ideation process. We'll make circles to start.

I encourage you, as much as possible, to accept and follow your own ideas. This can seem challenging, especially if you feel like you're not creative enough, or your skills aren't up to par. But creativity is a muscle. The only way you're going to get better, to feel more confident, is to exercise your imagination and build your skills. Any artist can show you work they made a decade ago, or even a year ago, and make a case for why their old pieces weren't up to the standards they have for themselves now. At the time, however, they were likely happy with what they made, and saw it as something they were proud of. Our progress is relative.

If you're feeling afraid, do it anyway. We'll start slow by creating "thumbnail" sketches that are a rough articulation of an idea. Then, we'll pick a concept (maybe two) and refine those into a more detailed drawing. At this point, color and materials get involved. By the time you're beginning to work on the final iteration of your project, you'll have a solid idea of what that will look like. Enjoy the act of making (put away that phone!) and be amazed at how it all comes together.

If you're feeling afraid, do it anyway.

Planning and Brainstorming

I find the brainstorming portion of a project the hardest part of it. It's here that you're figuring out what the thing will look like. Of course, that can change. Maybe you're the type that prefers spontaneity when you work. There is room for that, but having even a rough idea of what you'll create is helpful.

One trap that many people fall into is getting too attached to a particular part of a project. But when something about it isn't working—maybe the color isn't right or the shape looks funky—they don't want to change it because they are "too far" into the process, or too emotionally attached to what they've already made. This can happen at any point, but having a sketch usually helps you avoid this common pitfall.

Before you begin your sketching, select the format for your artwork. Because this is an embroidery-focused project, opt for a hoop. The size and shape are up to you; I used a 6-inch circular hoop. I like this size because it allows for more details than the 3- or 4-inch frames, but it's not so big that you'll be working on this project for years to come.

Keep some of these general composition tips in mind as you sketch:

- Refrain from putting your object in the center—especially if you're working in a circular hoop—to avoid the look of a bull's-eye.

- Think about adding diagonal lines for visual interest. (Diagonal lines help move our eye through the composition.)

- Ensure your picture is balanced by watching where the element is placed. If you have lines going off the top of the page, for example, have them leading off the bottom too.

- Empty space looks better at the base of the composition than at the top.

I like to start with the absolute, glaringly obvious basics and build from there.

Once you've determined your frame shape, grab your favorite pencil, sketchbook, or digital drawing tool. I began drawing on an iPad **(1)** with an Apple Pencil in 2019, and I've never gone back to drawing on paper. I use the Procreate app and for sketching use the program's "HB Pencil" brush to mimic the look of a pencil on paper.

To start, make four circles, squares, ovals—whatever the shape of your frame is. These will be your thumbnail sketches. Each one is a different concept. It's meant to be a rough drawing and contain the broad strokes of a concept and composition. Think about it as your thoughts on paper or screen. You can always create more shapes if you have more ideas.

Begin brainstorming by studying your object. Identify what it is. I like to start with the absolute, glaringly obvious basics and build from there. Using my treasure as an example, it goes something like this: I have a seashell. It's small, about 2½ inches long, and off-white in color. It has a spiral shape and an outer shell with a vertebrae pattern. I found it on a rocky beach while I was walking barefoot and getting my toes wet. The weather was cool, with some surfers and people flying kites.

This exercise can seem really basic and, frankly, feel like a waste of time. But when I acknowledge these things about the shell, it begins to conjure imagery and I understand what's important and exciting to me about the object. From there it's a natural progression to consider how I want to honor the shell, and what I want to say about it.

Back to your object. Maybe you have a shell, like me. Regardless of the item, start to draw your thumbnail compositions. It's tempting to go with your first idea, but your initial concept might not be your best. Make each sketch unique and treat each concept with the same reverence you give that favorite idea. One panel, for instance, could have a narrative bent to it. Another circle (or square or oval) could be more abstract. In each composition, be sure to indicate where the object will be placed.

Once you have four (or more) thumbnail sketches, determine which one is your favorite. Or, do you like elements of several sketches? You can always combine them; in that case, make another thumbnail sketch or two to see how it looks.

1

When you feel good about your rough sketch, it's time to start refining your drawing and planning for the final. Using the same format, make another shape that's much larger than your thumbnail sketches. Make it the same size as your embroidery hoop (if possible) for a one-to-one translation of the drawing to the final.

Your refined drawing should be a map for the final iteration of your piece. It should include finer details about where compositional components will go within its frame. In my drawing, you'll see that I have an emphasis on shape design. I think in shapes and like to break complex elements down into simplified forms.

At this point, you should have determined your artwork's concept. You'll now want to decide on the physical characteristics, including color and techniques, and start looking through your own materials to see what's feasible for your artwork. (It might require a trip to the craft store to bring your vision to life.)

The concept of my work is a loose interpretation of where the shell was discovered. I'm going to create a beach setting, but it's not going to be in a realistic style.

Rather, it will be stylized and focus on texture and pattern, using the appliqué technique. I think of appliqué as a fabric collage because pieces of textiles are arranged and sewn onto a larger backing fabric—not unlike a cut-paper assemblage. My plan is to use different types of fabrics, including cotton, linen, and felt, to create a scene that feels full and visually dense.

The shell is nestled within the sandy scene and surrounded by knotted embroidery stitches (including the French knot and some bullion stitch) to create some dimension. I did this because the shell itself will sit atop the fabric and stick out more than a lot of my fabric and stitches will. Adding these extra bits of texture marries the shell with the rest of the piece and makes them feel as though they belong together.

You don't have to have everything figured out by the time you finish your refined drawing. And you shouldn't; leave some things unknown. In that blank space is the opportunity to experiment and play. You'll cultivate an artistic voice that's faithful to you.

Practice Your Techniques

Every work of art is an opportunity to learn a new approach or way of working. Whether it's the first or 400th time you've done a technique, consider the ways in which you can make it new to you. (If it's your first time doing the thing, it is already new to you.) When thinking about your final piece, think about trying something different. Even if it's small—maybe you challenge yourself to try a new stitch or expand your color palette.

The final iteration of any piece is like the opening night of a play. You want everything to be perfect—for all the characters to say their lines correctly and for there to be no set or wardrobe malfunctions. Although you're not performing your art making in front of a crowd (most likely), it's hard to shake the desire of wanting everything on your first try. You'd never have to stop and rip a stitch or redo parts of your design. It's why sketching is valuable, and why practicing your techniques on scrap pieces of fabric is too. They're crafty dress rehearsals.

Whether it's the first or 400th time you've done a technique, consider the ways in which you can make it new to you.

My test piece is on the left, while the final version is on the right.

If it's the first time you're trying a new technique, good for you! Get comfortable with the approach by making a test, then evaluate how it worked. Is there anything you need to change? Are there things you could do differently next time? Make as many tests as you like, especially if you're still playing around with color. When you feel confident, you'll know it's time to move on.

Although you're not performing your art making in front of a crowd (most likely), it's hard to shake the desire of wanting everything on your first try.

Find a fabric base that complements your overall design.

Working on Your Final Piece

With your sketching done, your drawing created, and your techniques practiced, it's time to start on your final artwork. Start by taking your design and putting it onto your fabric. It's unlikely that everything in your drawing will make it onto the textile (remember, the drawing is a map), but you should block out the general points of your composition so you know where everything is going to go, and can ensure that all of the elements are proportional to one another.

For a design that's more involved, it's easier to trace it on the textile and then stretch it on the hoop. Size your design to the same dimensions as your hoop. You can redraw it at size, or if you drew it on a tablet, digitally resize it and print a copy of it out (this is what I did). A light box is ideal for this task, but if you don't have one, a sunny window will do just fine. Place your fabric atop your sketch and trace it, using a ballpoint pen. Once you're done, stretch it in the hoop and you're ready to get to work.

My design incorporates a lot of appliqué; it's how I formed the ocean waves, the trees, and the sandy bits. I cut those pieces out and stitched them onto the fabric stretched across the hoop. This will cover a lot of the backing fabric. Regardless of whether you're using the appliqué technique, I recommend finding a fabric base that complements your overall design. I stretched a sandy-colored felt in my hoop, with plans to add to it.

Consider the weight of your object when selecting your textile. My tiny shell isn't heavy, but I chose to use felt because it's thicker and stiffer. (Even with the felt, the extra weight is going to cause the fabric to sag slightly, so I'll apply a backing to the piece.) Are you going to apply paint to your fabric? This will also inform your textile choices. If you intend to paint with watercolor or acrylic paint, you'll want to select a fabric that will easily accept paint. In that case, cotton or a duck canvas is a good choice.

Before you begin working on your project, reassess the materials and techniques that you're planning on using. Generally, you'll want to work from the largest features to the smallest details of your design. If we think about the composition as layers, the biggest elements—such as the backing fabric—are applied first, while the tiny details—

such as accent stitching, for instance—are reserved to-ward the end of the project.

Your drawing will be helpful in determining the order of operations. If you're painting the background of your piece, apply the pigment first. Working with appliqué? Determine where the first layer of fabric will go, and attach that. Once you have the foundation of the piece done, build from there. Add more fabric, paint, or stitching until you've completed the small details that bring your piece to life.

Using Other Mediums on Your Fabric

It's possible (and encouraged, by me) to combine fiber art with other media. Paint, printing, beading, and drawing inks are just some of your creative options. Of potential media, paint is perhaps the most accessible since you could already have it in your home.

Painting your fabric is an effective way to cover large areas of your canvas without having to fill it with stitches. This makes it a great transitional technique if you're a painter who wants to try fiber art.

You can use watercolor paint or watered-down acrylic paint on the fabric. Unless your fabric is specifically primed for painting, however, your paint will soak into the fabric. (On treated fabric, your paint would sit atop it.) Fabric's absorbency will also cause the paint to spread, making it unpredictable with diffused edges. Because of this, try testing the paint on a piece of scrap fabric to see how it will react.

How to Appliqué

There are many ways to create an appliqué. Some people attach pieces to fabric by using a sewing machine or a stabilizing material, but you can do it sans a machine or additional supplies. All you need is a hand-stitching needle and thread that matches the appliqué piece you're going to attach (or doesn't match, if you're going for an accent look).

Fold, Press, Hand-Stitch (Needle Turn Appliqué)

The first method of appliqué assumes that you don't want a raw edge on the fabric that you're attaching. To avoid this, you'll need to fold the edges of the fabric and then stitch them onto your backing fabric. This is called needle turn appliqué. Begin by cutting the shapes out of the fabric, leaving a ¼-inch edge around the entire shape. Using an iron, press the extra ¼ inch to the back of the appliqué piece. (If you're working with a curved shape, you might need to clip the curve so that it lays flat.)

Flip over your appliqué piece so that the right side is facing you. The edges should be clean (because you've folded them in) and the shape should lay perfectly flat. Attach the shape to your backing fabric, using straight pins. **(1)** Alternatively, you can tack the piece by making a couple of stitches on either end and in the middle of the shape to hold it in place while you work. Do this in an area where you won't be stitching over. You'll remove the temporary stitches after you've secured the appliqué.

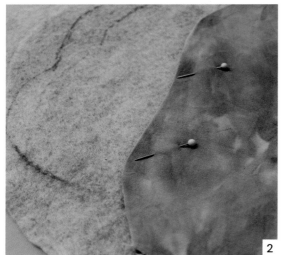

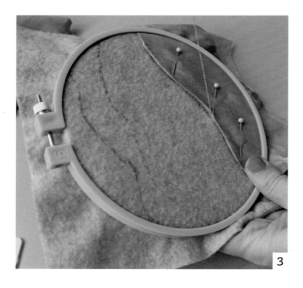

If you're applying a shape that goes off the edge of your fabric, you can keep those edges of it long enough to be secured in the sides of your embroidery hoop. **(2)**

With your shape now pinned or tacked, thread your sewing needle and knot the thread at the end. Then, bring it through the fabric underneath the appliqué (the base fabric) and then through the shape's creased fold. **(3)** The basic idea here is that, as a viewer, we won't be able to see the crease. By placing the stitch in the fold, you'll conceal the thread while still securing the appliqué and having a neatly finished edge. It's a win-win-win.

This step might take some finagling. I find that it's easiest to turn the hoop so that I am looking at the folded edge at eye level as opposed to above it. That way, I can see the needle go through the backing fabric and then exactly where it is in the fold so it will never be visible to the viewer.

Once you've finished your first stitch, move an ⅛ or ¹⁄₁₆ of an inch forward and repeat—go through the backing fabric and then through the fold. (This is a modified running stitch.) Continue to do that until you've reached the end. You might need to adjust your stitch length, depending on the shape. For tight curves, you'll want to make very short stitches so that the edge appears smooth. Stitches that are too far apart can look jagged.

Raw Edge Appliqué

Raw edges can be seen as something to avoid in fiber art. After all, if you're making something, the fraying can unravel all your hard work. But consider it from an aesthetic perspective; those same edges can add visual interest and offer an exciting juxtaposition to the clean lines elsewhere in your work. **(4, 5, 6)** I'm leaving my waves raw-edged and using embroidery stitches to tack them down. The unpredictability of a fray speaks to the ocean having a mind of its own.

Embracing a fabric's raw edges opens up even more possibilities for your image making. Although you can certainly outline the edge of the shape with stitching, try considering other ways you can stitch on top of it.

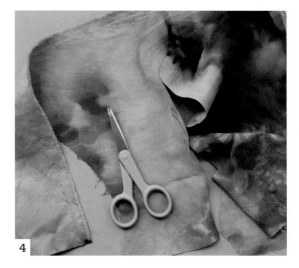

4

5

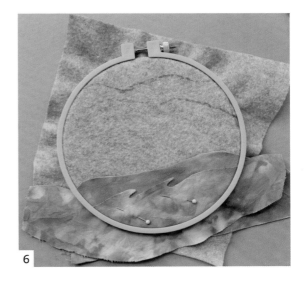

6

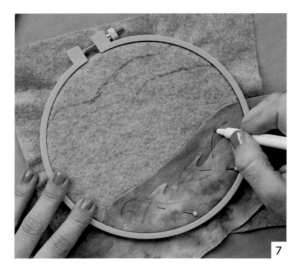

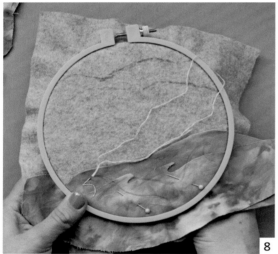

Embroidery Stitches

Split Stitch

I used embroidery to secure the waves but did so with ripple motifs created using the split stitch.

This is not a hard technique to replicate, and it's the part of the process where spontaneity comes in. I didn't have these particular waves in my refined drawing, but as soon as I cut out the fabric, it occurred to me that embroidery can add depth to the piece and secure it too.

This can be done either freehand or by drawing on top of the fabric for guidance. **(7)** I used a disappearing-ink pen to do this. This special pen is a fantastic way to draw atop the fabric in an impermanent way. The ink is formulated to disappear when it comes into contact with water. Or, if you don't wash it away, it will fade on its own in a couple of days.

Once I drew my design, I used the split stitch to trace my lines. **(8, 9)** I like using the split stitch because it mimics the chain stitch but is much simpler to execute. Start this stitch by bringing your knotted thread—that's at least two strands thick—through the back of your fabric to the front. Then, bring that first stitch forward as far as you like and then back through the fabric.

For all the stitches that follow, you're going to work forward and then backward. With your thread on the back of the embroidery, bring your needle past the stitch you just made and up through the fabric. Take the needle backward and insert it between the thread and pull it through. By doing this you're splitting the thread in and creating a chain-like effect.

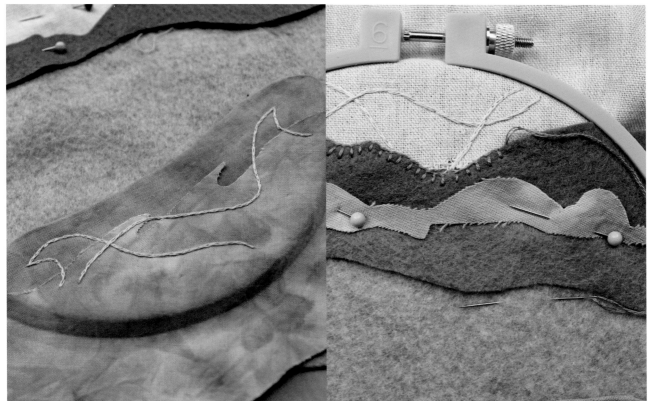

The split stitch adds a decorative element to the sky while the blanket stitch (page 23) secures the green felt.

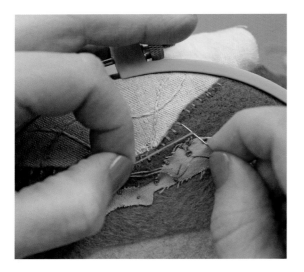

French Knot

Knotted stitches offer a texture that is great for re-creating grass, leaves, or any other element in which you want some dimensionality. The French knot is easy to replicate once you get the rhythm of it.

To begin, start with your hoop on your work surface—you'll need both hands for this technique. Bring your knotted piece of thread through the back of your fabric to the front. Then, using your nondominant hand (the one the needle isn't in), hold the floss tight and upright with your fingers a couple of inches above the hoop.

Turn your needle horizontally in your dominant hand and place it *in front* of the thread. Wind the floss around the needle twice and keep your wrist still as you do. Your other hand should still be holding the floss taut. The final step is to insert your needle, floss wrapped around it, into the fabric. Make a new hole in the fabric next to the original entry point. At this point, magic will happen: as soon as you pull your thread through the new hole, a small knot will appear.

If the knot looks messy, it might be because your thread was twisted when you wrapped it around your needle.

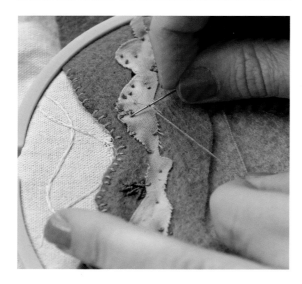

Bullion Knot

The bullion knot is another knotted stitch in which the thread is wound around the needle multiple times to produce a long, coiled stitch that sits atop the fabric. It resembles a tiny caterpillar, which is one of the nicknames for this fun technique.

The bullion knot is more complicated than the French knot, but knowing how to make it opens up more possibilities for three-dimensional stitching, including stump work (a type of three-dimensional embroidery in which designs are raised from the surface). The good news is that you use a lot of the same skills that you do when creating a French knot, so with a bit of practice, you should be able to make flawless bullions.

To make a successful bullion knot, you'll work from left to right (or right to left if you're left-handed) or up to down, depending on the direction of your stitch. Start by bringing your threaded needle up through the fabric. This is the first point of contact. Then, select the second point the distance in which you want the length of your bullion knot. If your knot is going to be horizontal, select the second point to the right of the first. If your knot is going to be vertical in your composition, make it below your initial point of entry.

Once you've selected how long your bullion knot is going to be, insert your needle and come up through the fabric very close (but not into) the first hole you made. Leave the needle in the fabric and hold on to it with one hand.

With the other hand, start to wrap your thread around the needle—as you did with the French knot—only this time, you'll wrap the thread enough times so that it's the same distance between your first and second points. After wrapping the thread around three, four, or five times (maybe more), pull the rest of the needle through the fabric. Continue to pull your thread until the coils lie flat against the fabric.

The bullion knot is a technique that often takes a few tries to master. One of the most challenging aspects of it is judging how many times to wrap your needle with thread. If you do it with too many or too few coils, your stitch won't lay flat. You'll also want to make sure that you don't pull your thread too tight or keep it too loose.

To add some visual variety to your knotted stitches, group bullion stitches and French knots along your fabric.

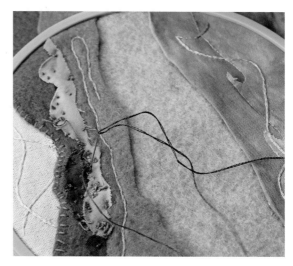

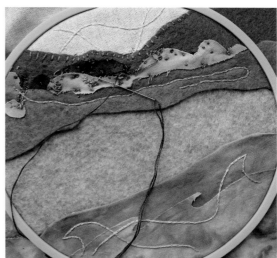

How to Attach Your Object

Attaching your object to your canvas should be one of the last steps. That's important to keep the integrity of your project intact—both your artwork "base" and the treasured object you've selected for it.

Many of the decisions about integrating your object with the rest of your textile art will depend on what it is. If you're incorporating a leaf, for example, you can stitch it directly onto the fabric by sewing over its stem and poking and stitching the fleshy part of it, similar to the work of Hillary Waters Fayle.

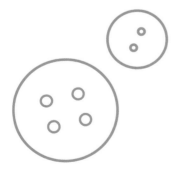

For something heavier than a leaf, you'll want to assess the best way to make sure it's both secure and doesn't weigh down your piece. Generally, you don't want to have something sagging in the center of your artwork; you want it to feel like it's fully integrated into your composition. I'm going to suggest something potentially scary—cut a hole in your fabric. This opening will be a place for your item to rest as it pokes through the back of your piece (which no one is going to see anyway).

Don't make the hole as big as your object. Rather, look at the part of the shape that protrudes the most, and cut a hole that the area can rest in. Depending on the size of the object, this might be an inch in diameter or less. With the hole cut, place the shape in the center of it. You should notice right away that while it still sits well above your fabric, it looks better integrated into the overall composition.

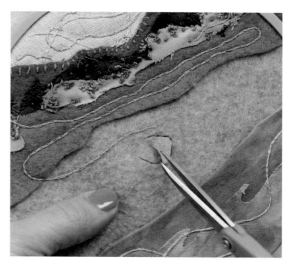

Because you now have a hole cut in your piece, you'll want to fortify the back. Cut a piece of fabric that is, ideally, the same as your base or backing fabric. (If that's not possible, it's okay. Just select something that is similar to your backing fabric so that it doesn't detract from your overall piece.) For me, it's a sandy-colored felt. It should be large enough to cover the hole that you just made, but you could go bigger to add extra stability.

After cutting the smaller piece of fabric, attach it to the back of the fabric you've stretched over your hoop. There are multiple ways to do this, and it will largely depend on the type of textile you're working with. Glue is one possibility. Hot glue is ideal for sticking felt together (this is what I used on the back of my project). If you are using cotton or a thinner fabric, opt for Tacky Glue. Its thinner consistency will ensure you won't see the backing fabric behind it. Tacky Glue will take longer to dry, however.

Alternatively, you could stitch the two fabrics together, using embroidery stitch as a decorative design.

Integrating Your Object with the Rest of the Piece

You've likely spent a lot of time stitching, appliquéing, and even painting your fabric—and that's before you placed your object in the composition. To make the item feel like its placement is purposeful, try incorporating elements around or even on it.

You likely planned for this in your drawing. I did; I wanted my shell to feel like it was nestled in the ground where I found it. But if you're stumped on how you'll marry artwork with your object, consider the overall concept of your piece. How important is it for the treasure to be integrated into your work? Some compositions might not require it; for instance, if they are very abstract. If your work skews narrative, it can be worth it—from a storytelling perspective—to integrate the unconventional item with your work.

This will likely require you to work some three-dimensionality into your piece. If the thought of that makes you queasy, I get it—a few years ago, I would've felt the same way. But it's possible to easily incorporate techniques

How important is it for the treasure to be integrated into your work? Some compositions might not require it.

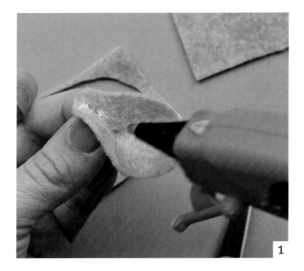

1

2

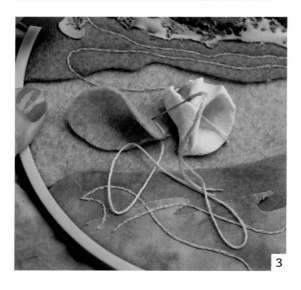

3

that will add dimensionality to your work. On my piece, I did this by cutting a piece of felt into roughly the shape I wanted my composition. (This is why I love felt—it has body, is inexpensive, and comes in many different colors.) I made sure to cut the shape a bit larger to account for the fact that it will be folded and sewn down, thus shrinking it a bit.

Part of the shape should be tacked onto your composition to give you the height you're looking for and to make it secure. To do this, pinch the end of your cutout and then run your needle through this section—a stitch or two should do. You can also glue it like I did. **(1, 2)** This will make your shape look like a flower petal. It will also give it some form and make it pop from your fabric.

If you're using cotton or any other fabric that frays, you'll want to make a choice at this point in the process: either fold the edges of the shape for a clean finish or keep the raw edge visible.

For a moment, let's assume that you're going with the raw edge (or you're working with felt). Take the part of your now petal that you just sewed and place it against your fabric. Holding it with one hand and a threaded needle in the other, make a whip stitch right against the edge of the shape and bring your floss over the pinched part of the petal. Insert your needle into the fabric on the opposite side. **(3)** Then repeat this a few times until the petal is stable. You will now have the part of the piece tacked onto your larger composition.

Now you'll need to sew the rest of the shape onto your piece. Fold the half-tacked shape over onto itself and use a straight pin to secure it. Make the stitch of your choice around the edge of the shape and into the base fabric. **(4)** Here, I again used the whip stitch.

A clean edge around your shape will look nice, but it will require an extra step. Begin by folding the raw finish so that it is now against the wrong side of your fabric. You can iron the edges in place, but this might be a difficult task if your shape is small. In that case, I recommend taking straight pins and pinning the folded shape to your composition. Then, using the appliqué technique discussed earlier, sew in the folds of the fabric and around the shape until it's fully joined to your artwork. **(5)**

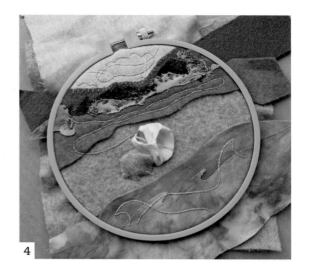

4

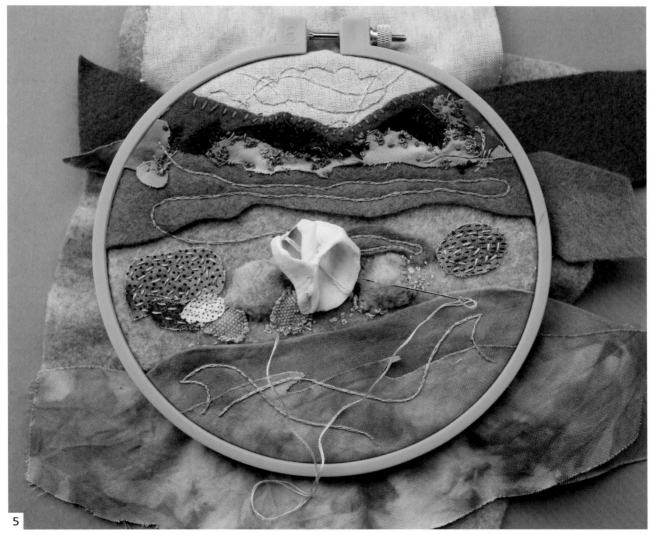

5

The Finishing Touches

Now, it's time for the final step—securing your hoop. You can display it in the hoop you're working in, which is what most makers choose to do. But if you're feeling a little fancy, opt for a frame specifically made for displaying embroidered artwork. These fixtures look like a conventional picture frame but are made with an inner ring that you put in place of your hoop ring and then work into. I'm using a decorative scalloped frame.

Regardless of the frame that you choose, you'll want to gather all the excess fabric that's outside your hoop, so that the whole thing looks neat, tidy, and professional. Fortunately, you can do this without the use of special clips or glue. You'll make a running stitch and cinch it all together like a drawstring bag before tucking it behind your frame.

Here's how to do it. Start by flipping over your finished piece, being mindful of the item you've so carefully placed on your fabric. Then, cut floss that's twice the circumfer-

ence of your hoop. Thread your needle and insert it about ¼ inch away from the edge of your hoop. Begin making a short ¼-inch stitch that's parallel to the hoop, but don't pull the string too tight once your needle is through the fabric. Keeping it loose, make another stitch that's the same length. Do this all around the hoop until you're back at your starting point.

Before knotting the thread and calling it a day, there's one final step to take: cinch the thread. Pull hard on your thread, and this will gather the fabric toward the center of your hoop. It's now ready to hang on the wall.

To take your finishing even further, cut out a felt circle and use the whip stitch to attach it to the back of your hoop. This will cover the backside of the stitching, also known as a #hoopbutt. Not all stitchers want to conceal this part of their hoop. Posting a #hoopbutt online is often a source of pride, whether it's humble-bragging how clean the wrong side of your stitching is, or how delightfully messy the backside has become.

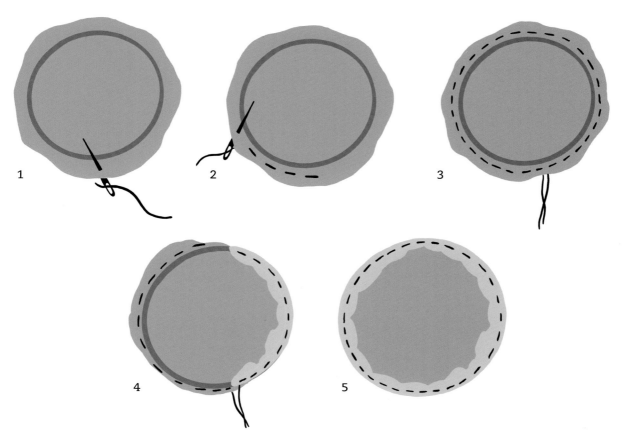

CHAPTER TWO

TREASURING THE THINGS WE LOVE

As we explored in the last chapter, treasure goes beyond jewels or precious baubles. Clothing and other wearables can be treasures too, such as a wedding dress that has been passed down for generations. But like Jessica Grady's love of everyday materials, seemingly ordinary garments are treasures when they're viewed in the right light and treated with the same respect and care we'd give to a fancy gown.

When was the last time you bought a brand-new—not just new-to-you—item of clothing? Maybe it's been awhile, or maybe it was just last week. But even if you've been able to hold off on buying a new shirt or pair of pants, mass marketing is often urging us to shop till we drop. This is at odds with what's best for our planet.

If we think about the whole of clothing production, from growing the fiber needed for raw materials to shipping from a factory to a fulfillment center, it is an environmentally exhaustive process. According to Earth.org, a not-for-profit organization that advocates for the protection of the environment (among other things), as of 2022, fast fashion generates lots of CO_2—more than aviation and shipping combined. About 20 percent of global wastewater is from textile dyeing, which contains toxic chemicals. Clothing production continues to fill our world with microplastics. And because we've been conditioned to wear the latest fashions, we discard a "garbage truck worth of clothing to the landfill every second."[1]

I find all of these statistics horribly depressing. And we can feel absolutely powerless in the face of fast-fashion brands such as Shein, which is "estimated to release 500 to 2,000 products every day,"[2] according to a 2022 article by Jake Silbert titled "Everyone Hates Shein but No One Wants to Stop Buying It."

But we do, of course, have a choice. We can choose to see items of clothing as investments that require long-term care. Clothing, while it helps us express ourselves, can also be a reflection of our larger beliefs and commitment to more-sustainable living.

Doing so requires a shift—of turning the dial from fast to slow fashion. There is more than one way to do this. You can shop secondhand or swap clothing with friends. You can make an effort to pick good quality over quantity, when possible, and repair things rather than discard them. You can give a refresh to clothing you find bland or unfashionable, whether that's adding adornments or altering it on a sewing machine to suit your taste.

This part of the book isn't going to give you tips on shopping secondhand. But it will get you thinking about how you can make your wardrobe a more sustainable one by way of mending, embroidering on clothing, and adding flair in the form of sewn-on patches.

I spoke with artists Arounna Khounnoraj, Tessa Perlow, Stefanija Pejchinovska, and Lindsey Gradolph about how slow fashion plays a starring role in their work. Whether it was out of necessity or to work against the status quo of clothing consumption, they each have ways to express themselves while making sure it's sustainable. They emphasize a connection to their garment or process and share how imbuing a bit of yourself into what you mend and stitch has benefits that extend beyond wearing the clothing.

The previous section of the book challenged you to create a work of art from scratch, essentially, inspired by at least a single object. Here, you're taking a different approach, but there are shades of similarity. You likely have an article of clothing in your closet in need of repair. You'll assess the garment and determine how you'd like to repair it and add your artistic flair to it.

There's a feeling of finality when mending or adorning clothing. Unlike artwork that you create from scratch, you can't completely start over if you don't like the direction your work is going. So that you keep the integrity of the garment, you have to problem-solve the moments that get tough. To minimize these moments—they are frustrating at best—I'll go over considerations to take into account as you cycle through ideas about how to transform your garment into something that's the star of your closet.

Imbuing a bit of yourself into what you mend and stitch
has benefits that extend beyond wearing the clothing.

Arounna Khounnoraj

Artist and author Arounna Khounnoraj began her fiber art practice by way of ceramics. With a background in fine arts, she spent a lot of her time in art school exploring sculpture by working with clay. But there was something about it that just didn't feel right, and by the time Arounna was in the midst of her graduate studies, she was struggling to create work that felt meaningful to her.

Similar to Hillary Waters Fayle (page 30), Arounna had the kismet-like experience of seeing how life can operate in cycles. Her professor posed a question that would lead her down a new—but familiar—path of making. Arounna's teacher asked what brought her the most comfort when she was a young person making art.

"The first thing that popped into my mind was working with my mother with textiles," she tells me during a video call in her studio in Toronto. Her family immigrated to Canada from Laos when Arounna was four years old, and her mom worked as a seamstress at a place called Tip Top Tailors. "She did piecework and so she was always sewing, and she made my clothes, and she taught me how to sew, and we were always doing some sort of activity together."

Arounna would pick out fabrics that her mom would fashion into outfits. As she thinks back on it, the experience created a "comforting connection" with textiles. But it wasn't an expression of creativity (although she was certainly being creative); her mom was making and mending out of necessity—as a way of making ends meet. "If kids saw you with a patch or a hole, they would just make fun of you and say you were poor." She would fix Arounna's clothing so that the repairs were invisible, to avoid her daughter being teased by her peers.

She would fix Arounna's clothing so that the repairs were invisible, to avoid her daughter being teased by her peers.

So imagine her mother's surprise when, many years later, Arounna's artistic practice would include mending clothing so that you see its worn journey. Through her work, a blown-out knee or tattered sleeve is celebrated as proof of it being well loved and something to honor.

Prior to mending, Arounna and her husband, John, began a studio called Bookhou—a combination of their two last names—and included things they produced themselves, from bags and pouches to furniture. They commit to a slow practice that centers on intention.

After 20 years, Arounna had a yearning to make one-of-a-kind work. It was at that point she began creating punch needle embroidery, which is a form of embroidery related to rug hooking. Instead of stitching through the fabric, you use a special tool—the punch needle—to push thread or yarn into the fabric. Although the technique goes back centuries, Arounna helped catapult the tool into the crafty zeitgeist in 2016, when a video of her using it went viral. This opened up doors for the artist. She authored a book on the subject, and it led her to share more of her practice and her wealth of knowledge.

With its special place in her life, mending gets to the heart of Arounna's studio. Fabric remnants are a great example of this. "[My] patchwork pieces were all based on this idea of trying to eliminate waste in the studio," she explains. "You're doing all this production work, and you have all these remnants, and you don't want to toss them."

Beyond the practical considerations, there are psychological benefits to repairing and reusing the items in our closets. Arounna sees mending as a form of celebrating the things that we already own and looking at them in a different light. "I always love that idea of how we connect to our things," she says. "I think it also relates to when I was watching Marie Kondo, and she was talking about does this thing spark joy? I think she was trying to communicate 'What connection do we have with it?'"

Mending is a way to renew our connection to a given piece. Because you spent so much time refreshing it, you couldn't possibly get rid of it now; it just feels right for it to be back in the rotation in your closet.

So many things in life are out of our control. You might be looking for a way to save money, or you just need a

You might be looking for a way to save money, or you just need a little "win" in your life. Repairing clothing does that.

little "win" in your life. Repairing clothing does that. You don't have to have any special skills to mend; all you need is a needle and thread.

The most straightforward technique involves a running stitch, and if you can do that, you can do a basic mend. "The idea of fixing a hole, it [gives people a] sense of accomplishment that they did something, and it didn't rely so much on their brainpower and became very meditative," Arounna explains. "It [is] really accessible, [and it gives people] a sense of control and a sense of peace and calm."

Mending really is as simple as picking up a needle and thread to fall in love with the process. I asked Arounna her favorite visible-mending approaches. "There's, there's so many," she says, before breaking down what she thinks is the easiest for someone who is just starting this sustainable practice.

Patching is at the top of her list. "You would take a piece of cloth, put it over the hole, and stitch around it," she explains. The technique has a long history; old textiles from India and Japan use patching on their woven fabrics. Patching is most often used on woven fabrics.

A patch is easy and efficient while offering seemingly endless opportunities for customization. "You could patch from the front," she offers, "you can patch from the back, [or] you can add interesting stitching, like you see with sashiko." Experiment with color and pattern. You can add stitching onto the design of a single patch, for instance, and have grow across your garment. "There are so many possibilities."

While there are techniques to learn, stitching can be personal. Don't be afraid to lean into it. "When you see somebody doing all these little stitches and mends, there's a real flow to it; there's a real rhythm to it that's really connected to them," Arounna says. "And it's just as original as their signature."

If you have some experience embroidering, consider what lights your fire and inspires you to stitch. It can likely be translated into mending. But if you're new to embroidery and mending, give some thought to what imagery you like and what you like to draw. Clothing is an extension of ourselves, and mending offers a way to imbue the things we own with more meaning.

Don't let your lack of experience or a creative block stop you from learning. Arounna sees herself as both a maker and educator, and she always wants to impress upon her students to have the confidence to try something new. "You shouldn't feel that you have to be in a certain niche," she says. "Just explore as many different things as often as you can, and you never know how those things will kind of inform what it is that you're doing."

Arounna uses her own experience with punch needle as an example. "If I wasn't open to using the punch needle, my work would have never changed from what it was before, where it was mostly printing and some embroidery. I feel that those paths that you take will definitely enrich and grow your practice."

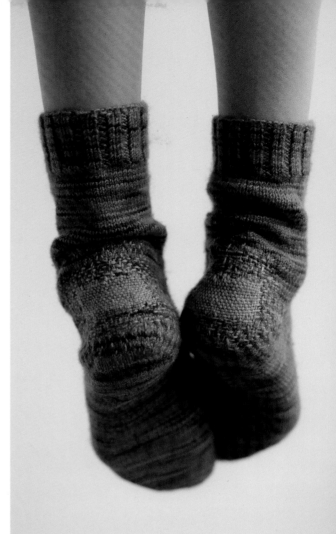

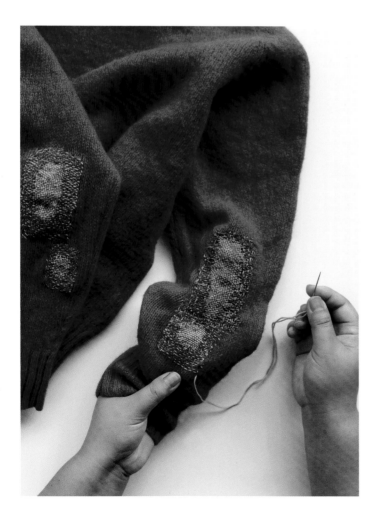

"You shouldn't feel that you have to be in a certain niche. Just explore as many different things as often as you can."

Tessa Perlow

Embroidery can turn an otherwise ordinary garment into a wearable work of art. For years, artist Tessa Perlow has taken secondhand garments and upcycled them into one-of-a-kind creations that convey her interest in books, tarot cards, flowers, and animals.

Tessa's early interest in fiber and textiles revolved around clothing. But rather than embroidering on it, she wanted to sew and make her own clothes. Her mom, a quilter, taught her how to sew, and she dreamed of being a fashion designer when she grew up; she adored costumes and movies. Tessa diligently honed her craft and often used hand-me-down clothing as the raw materials for her designs—unknowingly paving the way for her future career.

Tessa made it to art college, intending to do just what she had planned and major in fashion design. While there, however, her plans changed. Tessa realized that she didn't want to be in that part of the industry that contributed to the climate crisis and is known for exploiting workers. She also admits she's always had an independent streak about her, with a desire to work for herself.

"I've always been doing my own thing along the way, and I like keeping my own practice, even when I was in school," she explains to me from her Philadelphia apartment. "When I graduated and worked babysitting and food service jobs, I kept an art practice going." Taking this route has allowed Tessa to create work on her terms and fully explore her interests while still being able to pay her bills.

It's through these "random jobs" that she stumbled into embroidery and its easy mobility. "I was babysitting in Brooklyn and commuting from New Jersey, where I'm from," she recalls. "[Embroidery] was something that I could bring with me and keep busy, whether it's on the

train or sitting while the baby naps." This came at the same time that embroidery was having a renaissance and being firmly planted in the cultural zeitgeist; fashion houses such as Gucci were creating collections that included embroidery, and the enthusiasm caught on for independent makers like Tessa.

But unlike the fashion houses, Tessa didn't want to produce new clothing to put out into the world. She wanted to use embroidery to adorn the garments already out there—to upcycle them. She wanted to be prolific, but mindful of the environmental impact that her work had.

Tessa looks to thrift stores for clothing. "I'm pretty particular about sourcing garments," she explains. "I really want a garment that is going to stand the test of time." Quality makes a difference, especially because this is a second life for the piece of clothing. It's been washed and worn plenty of times before; can it stand up to the embroidery? "It might be a little more expensive, to get pieces that are fancier," she says, "but you know that they're going to be good quality, and you want to add really special work to it."

Upcycling presents a unique opportunity for a creative person. By working within the constraints of what already exists, you exercise both restraint and ingenuity. Restraint comes from embroidering in a way that adds to the garment and maintains its integrity and ingenuity, because embroidery can be used to cover up holes or permanent stains on the fabric. How the two work together is completely up to the artist.

Placement is an aspect of Tessa's work that's nearly as important as what she stitches. Long tunics have florals that meander up their sides and enhance the elongated proportions. A loose cotton blouse has a giant butterfly enhancing its boatneck collar. Each of her garments strikes the balance of being something she wants to draw (and stitch) while complementing their new canvas.

Every bold design is drawn freehand by Tessa onto clothing. "I'll sometimes use reference pictures, probably 50 percent of the time, especially to get the anatomy right on an animal," she explains, "or the color story of a butterfly." She's not always going for realism. And even if she is, it's important that she still draws directly onto the

garment, as opposed to other methods like a wash-away stabilizer. "I always want it to be freehand so that it's kind of imperfect and my own hand."

Many embroiderers will draw on fabric by using a pen, but Tessa has an alternative method. For lighter pieces of clothing, she uses colored pencils (she's fond of soft Prismacolors) to draw on the garments. If there are marks left after stitching, she will rub them away.

Darker fabrics are another story, as any embroiderer might know. "I was struggling to figure out what I liked the best for darker fabrics," she shares. "But now I like to use metallic marker pens." These types of utensils come in very fine tips, which allows for more-detailed draw-

"I always want it to be freehand so that it's kind of imperfect and my own hand."

"I was inspired by the idea of what a spell is and the elements that it could comprise."

ings. Tessa points out, however, that there is a caveat; you have to shake them before using them, and sometimes an errant ink drop will spot on the fabric, or an air bubble will form in the pen and mess up a line. That's where the beauty of Tessa's freehand approach works well. She simply adds to her design to cover up the new stains.

Embroidering on clothing is nothing new, but Tessa makes her work feel fresh, like you've never seen anything like it before, by having cultivated her visual language over time. One element of her stitching is harvesting imagery from her past work and figuring out how to do it again, only differently.

This is her go-to approach if she's feeling stuck or approaching a garment where she doesn't have anything in mind. She'll think, "I haven't really done flowers in a long time. What's one that I've never done before that would be an exciting thing to practice?"

Pushing your work forward—whether it's expanding what you draw or exploring one particular subject—requires consistent exploration. For Tessa, that means reading and studying subjects, outside of embroidery, that are of interest to her. She likes to dive deep. In 2020, she started reading books about tarot and magic in addition to nature and animal books.

"I was inspired by the idea of what a spell is and the elements that it could comprise," she explains, "and working on a piece as if it could be a spell, and [thinking,] "What are the ingredients in it?" The ingredients themselves inspire imagery while adding a personal and meaningful touch to the work. "A red candle could symbolize confidence, and so if I feel, 'Oh, I need more confidence this week,' I could [stitch] a candle."

Tessa admits she doesn't work this way all the time. After all, sometimes it's fun just to embroider a pretty flower without having to attach a deeper meaning to it all. But the act of ideation and the process she goes through to come up with concepts for her garments and hoop art help her dive deeper into her practice. Her imagery has an authenticity to it; when you see a piece by her, it's distinctive because it is a reflection not only of her technical skill but how her mind works. It is wholly her, even when her work is worn by someone else.

Lindsey Gradolph

For Lindsey and her embroidery, repetition plays a large role.

There was a time when the French horn was Lindsey Gradolph's future. Her parents encouraged her to pursue music at an early age, and she learned to play and perform well into her high school years. The plan was for her to play in college. But when the time came to go to her college auditions, Lindsey decided that she didn't want to play the French horn after all. (She hasn't played it since.)

Anyone who has ever learned an instrument knows the commitment it takes not only to be proficient but to be great. Mastering the French horn came at the expense of pursuing nearly anything else, and Lindsey realized she wanted to do more than play an instrument really well. At Georgia State in Atlanta, Lindsey was filling her requirements for an undergraduate degree, which included a language requirement. On a whim, she picked Japanese.

Japanese turned out to be more than just a one-semester class for Lindsey; she enjoyed learning the language and was naturally good at it. She went on an exchange program to Osaka for a year and eventually moved there after school to teach English in the Japan English and Teaching Program (JET). Lindsey stayed in Japan after the program was done, and has now lived in the country for more than a decade as an educator.

It's challenging to start completely from scratch, but it's also liberating. You discover your own way of doing things. For Lindsey, her foray into visual art as an adult began in Japan with watercolor painting. She painted for six years, and it was an exercise in pure creative expression without feeling the need to share online. She either gave the works to friends or threw them away. But while painting, she used Instagram and Pinterest to help discover artists

and develop her vocabulary for talking about them.

"To be 26 years old and discover names everyone knows, like Louise Bourgeois . . . ," she recalls to me from her apartment in Tokyo, "I went down a rabbit hole."

You never know how inspiration will manifest itself via the things we're interested in. For Lindsey and her embroidery, repetition plays a large role. "I've always loved repetition," she shares, "and the accumulation of repetitious things. I love Philip Glass and that kind of music with really intense droning-like sounds." It's the accumulation of visual elements that excite her. "I really like color, and form, [such as] geometric shapes. I like how they relate to each other and how small things over time can build up to something really cool; I think it's quite fascinating."

Lindsey's paintings were abstract and consisted of wavy lines that built on each other. Once the lines were dry, she punctuated the "rainbow vibes" by making smaller markings over the painting with a black pen.

Lindsey eventually abandoned watercolor. (Like her decision with the French horn, she hasn't painted since.) But we contain multitudes, so her exploration into making wasn't all about painting. Even before she began painting, she was interested in slow fashion. By 2012, the slow fashion movement was out of obscurity and gaining traction in popular culture. Where there was once a stigma around secondhand, thrifted clothing was now seen as "cool."

Working from patterns, Lindsey began sewing her own garments, but it was short lived. One of the goals of the slow fashion movement is to curb overconsumption. After making some clothes, she realized she didn't need to add more to her wardrobe, and accumulating more clothing in her Japanese apartment made an already small space cramped.

The watercolor painting and clothing construction, however, was an unlikely duo that led Lindsey to begin embroidery. Painting helped her define her visual language, while sewing gave her a mechanism for a new way to express it.

"I knew of what embroidery was, [that it uses a] hoop and thread and needle," she explains. "But some of those things weren't really easy to get in Japan, or at least they

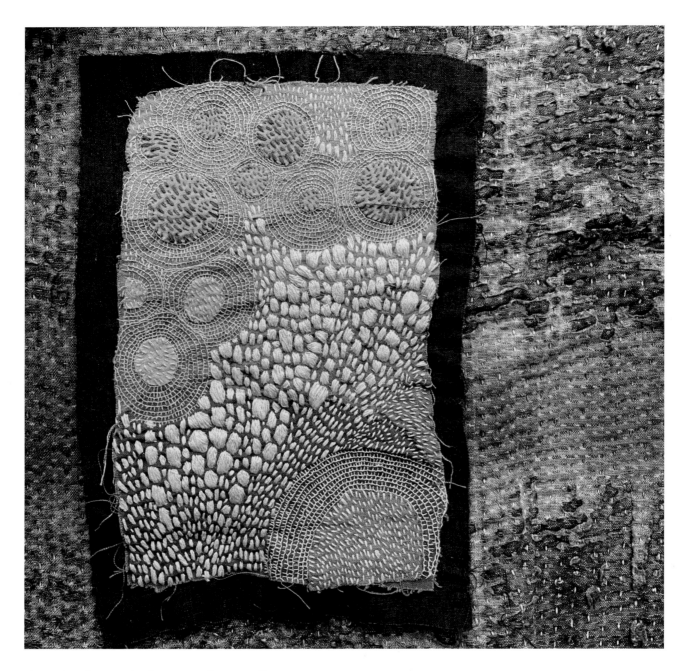

"That's where I think my work came from: being really inspired by quilting, but having no patience for it."

weren't eight years ago when I first started." DMC thread, a go-to thread for many stitchers, was expensive, and other colorful thread was not easy to access. The barrier to supplies didn't stop her from pursuing the new-to-her craft, though, and she started embroidering using button thread that's the same weight you'd use in a sewing machine.

Beginning embroidering opened up a whole new world for her. It was around this time that she discovered sashiko and boro. Sashiko is a technique that involves fortifying a garment while adding decorative stitched designs. Boro refers to the result of repetitive sashiko on the same item throughout time (sometimes many generations).

Lindsey is quick to point out that while she likes and appreciates sashiko, her work is not sashiko. "The one thing I'm inspired by in sashiko is the contrast of the blue and the white," she explains. "I admire it, but I never tried to emulate it or do it myself."

Lindsey embroiders on secondhand fabric, and it's plentiful in Tokyo. People sell fabric by the kilogram, and Lindsey buys scraps of indigo fabrics. "There's nice sun fading," she says. "It's a grab bag of surprises." Fisherman flags are an unlikely but useful material for her too. "[They have] primary colors I like, and so I find those—they're vintage—but I'll cut into those to use as a color palette. I really love high-contrast colors, and the white thread over it is additional contrast."

Lindsey's love of repetition and penchant for taking on time-consuming tasks yields bold embroidery—thanks to choice in color palette—that is covered in texture. She varies her mark making, which allows our eye to bounce from concentric rings to scale-like coverings and never get bored.

Below her intricate stitching are fabric shapes inspired by quilters. But, as Lindsey points out again, they aren't quilts—although she's found inspiration in the practice. An exhibit of works from the Gee's Bend Quilters was particularly powerful, and Lindsey admires the contrast and patterns in their designs. Lindsey, however, can't see herself being a quilter. "I don't have the patience, at all, to quilt. I don't like reading instructions. I don't like following a pattern." She liked how the quilts looked, but decided to replicate the aesthetic on her own.

"That's where I think my work came from," Lindsey says. "Being really inspired by quilting, but having no patience for it." She'd cut the fabric into pleasing shapes, arranging them into the little landscapes on her base fabric. "That's where the embroidery came from," she reveals, "[because I] have to make sure it all stays together."

Creating her stitched designs starts in her head. "Often, I'm thinking as I'm working on something, 'I want to

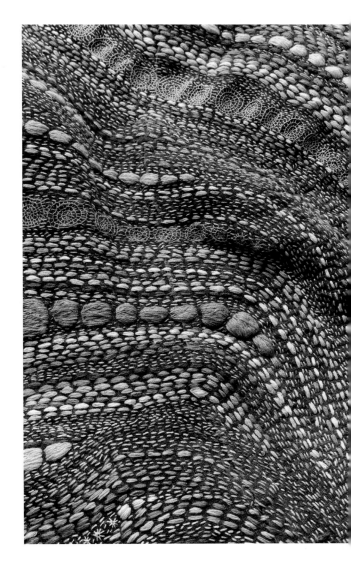

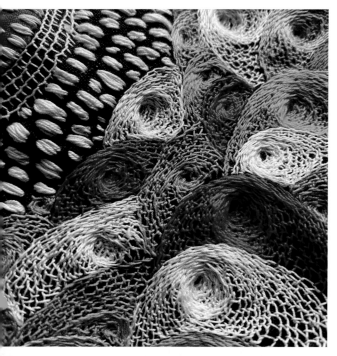

do this next.' And so I'll sit there and obsess about it." By the time she sits down to stitch, she has a general idea of how she wants the piece to look. Despite her fabric being covered in linework, she doesn't draw the design out ahead of time. Rather, Lindsey thinks about water and how it flows. "I always start in one part and make an additional line. And then from that line, it's like, well, it just kind of flows out from that initial point."

Very rarely does Lindsey remove stitches. If she makes a mistake, it stays, and it ultimately evolves her surface design. Examples are pieces that include white, bubbly dots. When Lindsey first made these marks, it was because a line wasn't flowing with the composition exactly how she wanted. So, she continued to sew over it to make it go away. The blob grew, and she figured she'd better make another one next to it. She's incorporated them in many additional pieces ever since.

Whether it's sashiko or quilting, traditional fiber arts are the jumping-off points for Lindsey. While some of these techniques might be reminiscent in her work, she's made them all her own.

Just as she decided to forgo the French horn many years ago, Lindsey has done the same with her art. It's taken years to get there, but that's the thing about creative work. "If you want something to be the way you want it to be, you actually have to spend the time to do it," she says. "There's no cheap way out. It's easy to commodify things, and some things can't be commodified. I think that's why I enjoy my work."

At one point in our conversation, Lindsey referred to herself as a "tornado person" who is stubborn. Her pieces, in contrast, are calm in that storm. They offer peace and tranquility. "Two different Japanese people said that my work reminds them of a Zen rock garden," she says near the end of our chat, "which I think is pretty accurate. In this space, I control everything."

Stefanija Pejchinovska

Stefanija Pejchinovska, who works under the name Damaja, was supposed to be an architect. And she was, for a while. But her studies and career meant spending a lot of time in front of the computer, and she needed something to do to occupy her hands. Embroidery was a natural choice for her. She had observed her crafty grandmother stitching (although she never taught Stefanija how), and she took it up as a craft when she was about eight years old. "It wasn't like embroidery was trendy," she tells me. "I was just doing it all my life."

Stefanija was born in Macedonia and was living there when she opened Damaja Handmade on Etsy. It was soon a successful business for her. So successful that she quit her architecture job after about two years and decided to move to Berlin, which is where I spoke with her. Stefanija has been in Berlin since 2016 and started embroidering on clothing at that time.

Stefanija imbues garments with her unique visual language. The stitched imagery often combines abstract and figurative elements. A bowl of fruit is placed alongside squiggle lines and a stylized eye. Together, the elements read like a puzzle, where you're trying to put together what each means and how it relates to the other. They are alluring in their inscrutableness, which speaks to her desire to make something that feels wholly original.

Cultivating this type of visual voice takes a sustained effort that isn't as easy as it might sound. Many artists know this well; Pablo Picasso epitomized it in a famous quote of his: "Inspiration exists, but it has to find you working."

"You need to spend time working on a design," she explains. "Of course, ideas come in the shower, or when you

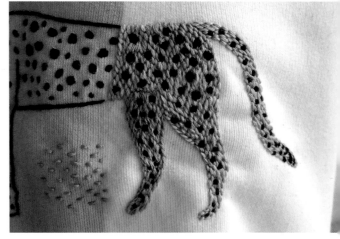

see a movie, or when you hear some song. But you have also got to train your brain to think like that." Learning to recognize what interests and what inspires you is important, while also being aware of how these influences can play a larger role in your embroidery.

While it's helpful to know what your contemporaries are creating, it can be dangerous. If you're looking at what people in your same field are doing, and making work based on that, there's a danger of replicating their work with a lack of authenticity in your own.

For this reason, Stefanija doesn't look at other embroiderers for inspiration. "If I see something that's good, why would I want to do that [in the same way]? That's why I always get inspiration from anything else, from photography, even just objects like vases, but I never ever look at other people [for inspiration]." When she does view the work of other fiber artists, it's out of admiration and nothing more.

There is a structure and an order to Stefanija's embroideries that reveal her architectural roots. Details of the compositions are organized like the blocks on buildings and read as a blueprint to her mind. The individual elements might seem as though they have little in common, but each two-dimensional assemblage is carefully considered.

"I see [my embroideries] like collages," she explains. "I don't draw that much in notebooks. I just draw directly onto the clothing, but I make only outlines. I paint with the threads. I don't know from the beginning how my embroidery will look."

This is where the collages are helpful. Her ideas can come from many places. "It can start from seeing objects in the room I am in, or outside the window, or something I saw that day, something I read or see when I go on Pinterest." Her saved posts on Instagram are also a source.

Stefanija will take her favorite components and start to arrange them. This is without the use of any planning tools like Photoshop; she does it all in her head. She will place a garment on a table and begin to envision how it will look with her added stitching.

In addition to drawing, selecting colors is another important part of her process. Stefanija uses the thread-painting technique, and finding the right hues can

"Of course, ideas come in the shower, or when you see a movie, or when you hear some song. But you have also got to train your brain to think like that."

be a challenge. The goal is for her different flosses to appear to blend into one continuous color.

"Nobody knows how much it takes time to combine colors so [that] they actually fit [together]," she sighs. "Even if it's one shade [different] from the one that you need, it's just not the right one, and then you can spend half an hour searching for the right shade."

Placement is also an important part of Stefanija's work. Her designs are often small and don't cover a large surface area. But when stitched on a sleeve cuff or trailing down the side of a top, they make a big impact while being subtle too. "Embroidery takes a lot of time," she points out, "and you have to be smart." She opts for positioning that feels organic, and likes to stitch around edges or make designs look as though they are emerging from the placket of a button-down shirt.

Although Stefanija isn't sure how the embroidery will look once she begins, she always has an uncanny sense of when it's complete. "You see it from afar and [know] something is missing," she explains. "Even if I have to add just two stitches, I know they are missing. And when I add them I know it's done."

Stefanija regularly teaches embroidery workshops in Berlin, and she instructs her students to start with fabric like cotton or linen for their first stitching projects. Jersey or stretchy textiles are harder to learn on. "First, you have to get a sense of the fabric and of the threads—how they fit together, how much you should pull on them—and with T-shirt knit, it's not the same."

It might be hard to imagine what your embroidery will look like when you first draw on that design, but Stefanija is confident it will look good. "I say to everyone, whatever you do with embroidery, [that] the moment you add stitches and texture, it's going to be nice. There is no way to make something that's not nice."

"Even if I have to add just two stitches, I know they are missing. And when I add them I know it's done."

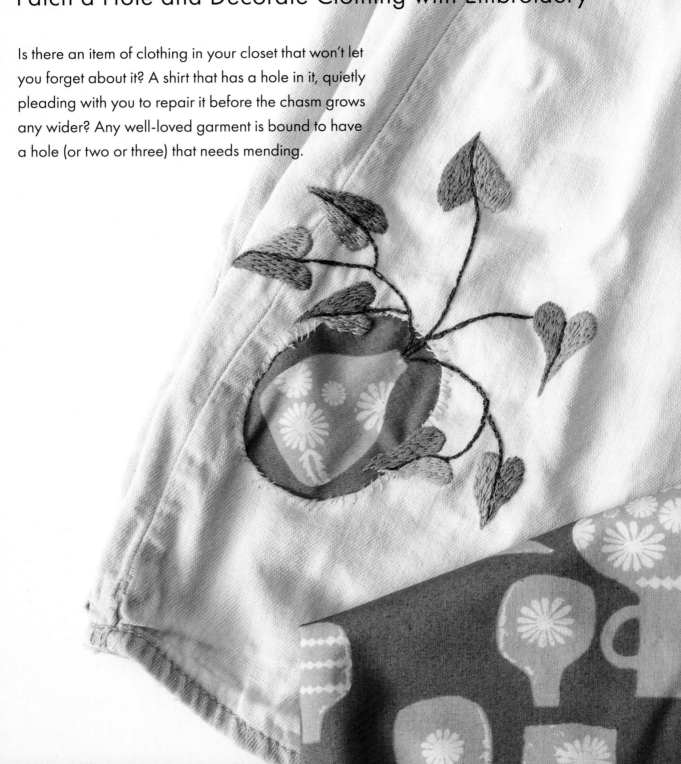

Patch a Hole and Decorate Clothing with Embroidery

Is there an item of clothing in your closet that won't let you forget about it? A shirt that has a hole in it, quietly pleading with you to repair it before the chasm grows any wider? Any well-loved garment is bound to have a hole (or two or three) that needs mending.

If you've been putting it off, now is the time for repair. And not only that, but to look at this as an opportunity to write a new chapter in this garment's history.

You might have a collection of clothing that's in your "someday pile." Someday you'll have the time, the creativity, the skills to mend that special garment and put it back in the rotation in your closet. I'm here to tell you that "sometime" has come. Visible mending is both a practical and creative endeavor that can be as fulfilling as other projects. Plus, there's a bonus when you repair something—you get to wear it again!

My process for mending is not unlike the one I shared in chapter 1. There is planning involved. While you might want to adorn a garment à la Tessa Perlow, if you're planning on repairing an article of clothing (and not just embellishing it), you'll want to carefully consider the steps you'll take to do so. The ultimate goal of mending is to prolong the life of a garment through repair. Some planning is essential to ensure that you keep the integrity of the fabric so that your garment is better for it.

Planning and Brainstorming

Even if you're not the planning type (tell me, what is it like in your world?), there are some baseline considerations to take into account before you apply patches and embroider designs onto the garment you intend to mend. Chances are you've already thought about some of these things as you were adding a garment to your repair pile.

What Is the Material of Your Garment?

You set your garment up for success when you incorporate similar fabrics in your repair. The most common thing you'll be repairing, most likely, is woven (such as a button-down shirt). If you're patching, select a woven fabric for it. If you're repairing a hole in a sock or sweater, try darning with yarn. The garment will move better and be more stable when you repair it.

How Will Mending or Adorning Change How You Wear the Garment?

Mending and adorning clothing is an opportunity to change how it's perceived by others. It opens the door to

Mending and adorning clothing is an opportunity to change how it's perceived by others.

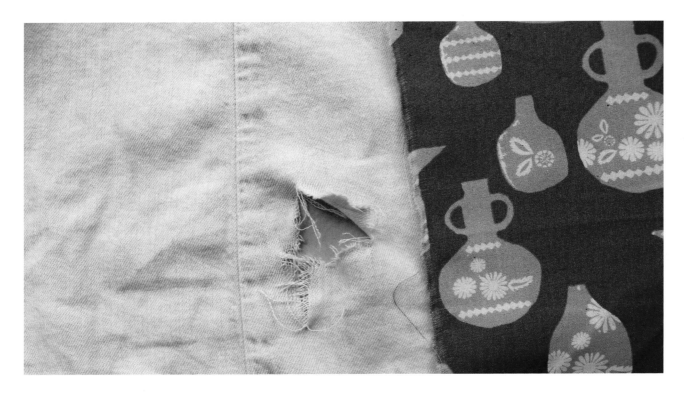

The hole is the visual anchor for my new design.

clothing that has a lived-in feel but is refreshingly brand new. This is particularly true when you stitch a design onto clothing. Adding embroidered imagery onto a shirt can make it look fancier than when you began. Consider where you wore this garment before your customizations, and brainstorm new ways you can show it off when you're done. With certain additions, there are possibilities for this garment to shine in a wider variety of social situations. Your changes might also change how you wear the article of clothing. If you add embroidery to a part of the shirt you'd usually tuck in, you probably won't want to do that anymore.

How to Approach Your Garment

Once you've selected your garment and have a general idea of the direction you're going to take it—whether that's mending, adornment, or a combination of the two—start planning how you're going to work on it. It's not a requirement when you're mending, of course, to stitch a design that interacts with that mending. But in the story that the garment tells, the two offer a creative way to do so.

For my purposes, I have a well-loved chambray shirt that was given to me as a gift nearly a decade ago. It's soft and has multiple holes—one of which was on the front of the shirt, near the bottom of it. I patched under the shirt to cover the hole and then used that as an opportunity to decorate the shirt with embroidery and attach patches that I created. The hole is the visual anchor for my new design. Because it was the bottom of the shirt, there wasn't much place to go but up.

There are multiple ways to plan how you'll adorn your garment. In my case, the patching was fairly straightforward. Because it was patched under the garment, there isn't too much more to consider beyond the color and pattern of the fabric I used. But be mindful of your materials and consider new ways in which they can inspire you. I bought the fabric at my local craft store, and it's designed by Ruby Star Society, known for its unique surface patterns. It has vases printed all over it.

The fabric's surface design provided inspiration for how I embroidered the rest of the shirt. I wanted to bring the spirit of the vases onto the garment, so the illustrations I created were related to the pattern while also adding my spin to it. Inspired by what goes into a vase—flowers and other greenery—my design would also include botanicals.

What can your fabric tell you? If you're using printed pattern fabric as I did, yours too can serve as inspiration for how you adorn your shirt. Alternatively, you can pick a solid fabric in a shade similar to your original garment. Opting for subtlety, you could stop at the patch or take the color-matching even further and play with tone. If stitching on a denim shirt, for instance, you'd use a slightly lighter or darker blue to add a design that, while not quite a statement maker, imbues your clothing with personality.

There's one more thing I added to my shirt: a felt patch. Embroidered patches like this are my favorite way to add a little something special to a garment. You can apply a patch to a new or older article of clothing, and it doesn't need to be large or the design to be overly complicated to make your garment pop.

Embroidered patches are my favorite way to add a little something special to a garment.

Play with Placement

You now have an idea of what you're going to do to the shirt. Now, it's time to figure out where your design (or designs) will be placed. As we've seen in the work of Tessa and Stefanija, the placement of embroidery or a sewn-on patch can have a big impact on the vibe of your overall piece.

Embroidering something too high or too low on a garment can make beautiful work look awkward when worn. Alternatively, it can be a way to add playfulness to your clothing when paired with certain types of subject matter. An animal being placed above the pocket looks like it's sitting inside your shirt, for example. Florals can be a way to add visual interest and call attention to certain areas of a garment. The area you dream of accentuating (or even hiding, such as that awkward stain that won't go away) can be covered with stitching or patches.

Scale is different than placement, but the two work closely together. Something very large—over the chest, for instance—can visually overwhelm a garment. But that might be the point; you're going for something that people can't help but comment on when they see you. When considering the size of your embroidered additions, remember that a smaller scale can embrace subtlety, or be a way to make a big visual impact by replicating it many times throughout your garment.

Make a Plan (or Wing It)

Planning your design can be challenging and even a bit tedious at times. But when you're working on something that you can't easily start over on (such as a piece of clothing), the time spent sketching is worth it.

I'm not quick at thinking on my feet (don't ever ask me to take an improv class), and I love an agenda. Before I put stitches to fabric, I have a plan for how it will look. A lot of detail isn't required, but I recommend starting work on your garment with a general idea of placement, colors, and the stitches you're going to use to bring your work to life. It can be on paper or digitally, or, as Lindsey has shared, you can always create the "sketch" in your head.

(For help in brainstorming ideas, refer back to the "You Can Do It" section in "Displaying Treasures.")

Start your work with a general idea of placement, colors, and the stitches you're going to use.

How you do this can take multiple forms. I'm fond of mockups, and I snapped a photo of the shirt (with the patch), imported the image in Procreate on my iPad, and drew it on top of it. This allowed me to try out different designs and configurations without the risk of making permanent marks on the fabric.

This might not be an option for you. If you still want the benefit of planning what you're going to stitch, a pencil and paper will help you plan. Even having a rough idea of what you want to embroider can provide more confidence in what you're applying to the fabric. Try sketching the designs at scale whenever possible. You can cut them out and lay them on your garment to see how they will look. Move them around to determine the perfect spot and if they're the right size. You might find that making an illustration smaller or larger is a more aesthetically pleasing choice.

Once your designs are ready, trace over them by using a ballpoint or gel pen. And as Tessa showed, colored pencils will work too.

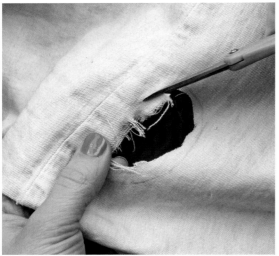

Transforming Your Garment

When transforming a garment, mending comes before adding embroidery. Doing so will help stabilize your shirt or pair of pants. It's much easier, after all, to stitch on fortified fabric than it is to navigate around loose, floppy holes.

There are two ways to patch a hole: on top or below.

Patching a hole on the top of the fabric is generally the simpler of the two techniques. With this approach, you will cover the hole by adding your new fabric to the outside of the garment. This allows you to experiment and play with the shape of your patch. You could, for instance, create a patch that is just large enough to completely cover the hole. Alternatively, you could cut fabric that's much larger than what you're mending. It'd add a statement-making element to your garment.

Once you've considered size, determine how you will finish the edges of your patch. You can leave the fabric's raw edges and attach it to your garment using a running stitch or a whip stitch. (Keep in mind that as you wear the clothing after you patch it, the raw edges could fray.)

Another method is to clean-finish the edges of the patch before you sew it onto your clothing. Do this by folding and pressing the raw edges of the patch to the fabric's backside. Then, using the stitch of your choice, sew the folded edge in place. Now that your patch has a clean finish, attach it to your garment by using a running stitch or a whip stitch.

Patching a hole below is similar to affixing fabric on top of the garment. But instead choosing the size and shape of your patch, working beneath the hole is dependent upon how big the tear in your fabric is.

Before beginning, consider if you'd like to leave a raw edge of the hole or if you'd prefer a clean shape. Both are suitable for patching, so this is purely an aesthetic choice.

Regardless of the edging, cut your patch fabric bigger than the hole. Opt for a square or rectangle.

If you're leaving the raw edge of the hole, you don't have much more to do. Hold the patch in place by using a running stitch around the hole.

If you're opting for a clean finish, first determine your shape by outlining the hole. I used a disappearing-ink pen, but you could use a pencil or chalk. This will be the new edge of the patch.

Because I had specific plans for my patch fabric (I wanted the full vase to be visible), I cut the hole a little larger to accommodate the design.

With your outline drawn, create notches around that outline by making small "V" shapes; doing this will help keep a smooth curve around the clean edge. Start stitching around the hole by tucking the fabric underneath and using the whip stitch.

The final step, regardless of whether you chose a raw edge or a clean shape, is to further secure your patch while celebrating your mend. Use a whip stitch around the outer edge of the patch. Match colors for a subtle appearance or accent the patch with a different hue.

(I skipped this step because I was embroidering a design onto the patched area that secured it.)

Once your patching is complete, grab your embroidery essentials to start stitching on a garment. Identify where you'll place your design, and freehand draw it on the garment with a disappearing-ink marker, colored pencil, or ballpoint pen.

If you're thinking, "I don't want to draw on my fabric! What if I make a mistake?," know that I'm the same way. There are a couple of options for calming this fear. One is to accept that you might flub a pen line or draw something that looks a bit wonky. Being open to this as a possibility, before you even begin, can take the pressure off having to perfectly draw your design. You can decide to just go with it. Tessa and Lindsey have shared ways in which they account for errors; Tessa simply extends her design to cover blunders, while Lindsey will try to change the misstep with more stitching. You can look at this as an opportunity to learn more about your materials and even to see how this tiny change can set your work in a previously unexplored direction.

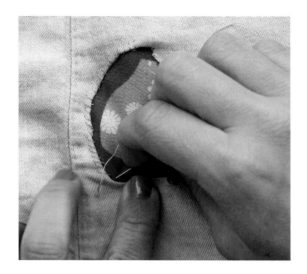

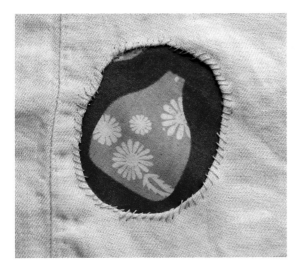

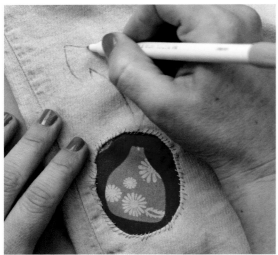

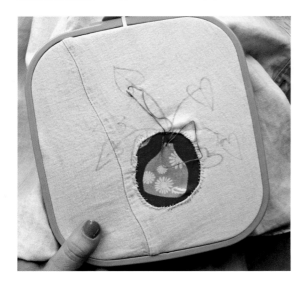

Another option is to use a product called stabilizer. Stabilizer is often used in garment construction and other sewing applications, but it's also valuable for hand embroidery. In fact, this is what I used for my sewn-on patch. There are different types of stabilizers—cutaway, tearaway, and wash-away. To use stabilizer, digitize your design and have a printer handy. When you've finalized what to stitch, simply insert a sheet of the stabilizer into your printer and print the design.

Cut out the design from the stabilizer sheet, leaving a little border around it, and affix it to your fabric. The way to do this will depend on the type of stabilizer that you're using. Wash-away stabilizer, for instance, is stick on, while cutaway and tearaway require you to baste or hoop it into place. (Be sure to read the manufacturer's instructions for using its stabilizer.) Once you're happy with the placement of your design, start stitching as normal.

With your design on the fabric, start by placing part of it in an embroidery hoop and selecting your thread. Then, it's as simple as incorporating your favorite stitches into the design. (Okay, let's face it—that is way easier said than done.) Depending on the level of detail and size of your image, you'll want to consider how many threads are in your needle. I typically stitch with two threads because it offers a lot of control when working on intricate designs. But for something much larger, you might work with four or more strands of thread. This will make your stitching go faster, but you'll achieve less detail.

Also consider the length that you make each stitch. Opt for stitches that are shorter in length, since the fabric will be bending and moving. If a satin stitch is a few inches long, for instance, it won't move with the fabric. Using shorter stitches, such as a shortened satin stitch or the long-and-short stitch, will prevent the thread from coming off the fabric anytime it's not laid flat.

When you're done with your embroidery, remove the stabilizer. For wash-away varieties, you will run the design under warm water to loosen the stabilizer and remove it from your garment. Rinse well to ensure that the stabilizer is fully removed from your design. The excess cutaway and tearaway is removed after you're done.

A stabilizer is handy because of the control it affords

you, but it's not without some downsides. One of them is environmental; this method is not zero waste. There are always stabilizer scraps, and the wash-away method sends plastic residue down the drain.

The other is that it can change the feel of your threads. Because the stabilizer is a firming agent, your threads won't be as soft and fuzzy as before washing away the product. But this is also helpful—especially if you're planning on wearing the garment a lot—because it will ensure that the design stays in place and is less likely to snag.

Depending on the level of detail and size of your image, you'll want to consider how many threads are in your needle.

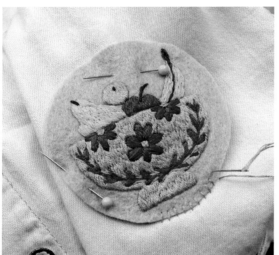

Creating a Sewn-On Patch

While we often think of patching as covering a hole, that's not always the case. It can be a purely decorative element affixed to any part of a garment—whether it has a hole in it or not. This adds some playful possibilities. Patches offer an easy way to cover a stain or permanent mark. You will also work on the patch independently of the garment, offering you some flexibility in how and where you work on it.

Regardless of your design and how you transfer it, stitching onto felt is the easiest way to make a sewn-on patch. Felt comes in a variety of colors and is an inexpensive material. Best of all, it won't fray because of its interlocking fibers.

Embroider your imagery by using your favorite stitches. When you're done and ready to attach it to your clothing, cut around your design. You can follow the shape of the embroidery or trim it into a circle, oval, or any other form your heart desires. Leave at least ¼ inch around the edge for attaching it to the garment. Once you're done trimming, use a running stitch, back stitch, or whip stitch to secure it on your clothing.

You're now ready to rock your garment, but remember you don't have to stop there. You can continue to add to it and continually reinvent its look time and again.

Finished! For now. Remember that you can reinvent your garment's look time and again.

CHAPTER THREE

TREASURING EVERYDAY MOMENTS

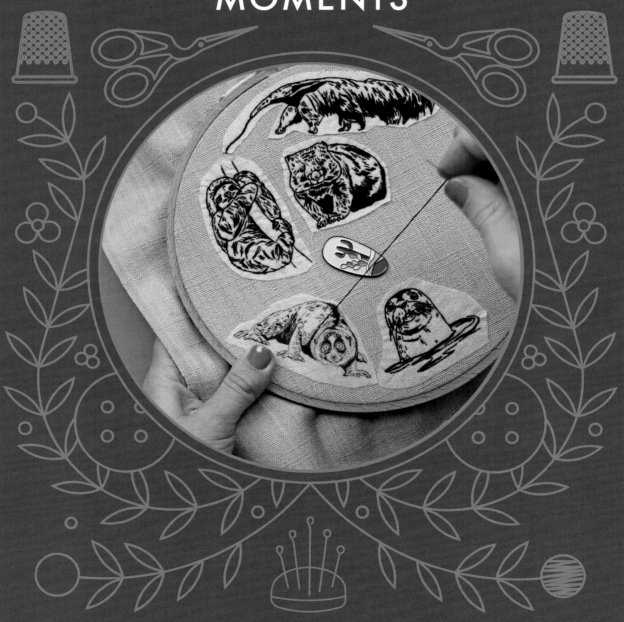

If we're lucky, there is a predictable rhythm to each day. The steam rising from a cup of coffee; the symphony of phone notifications; the crackle of oil in a frying pan. To some, it might be mundane. But these habits and routines are a vital part of our existence. Together, they imbue our lives with meaning.

We can reframe the everyday from being something that we simply endure into something that we can cherish. Of course, that's not easy with everything in life. There are some tasks that no amount of reframing can help. We may have to clean up after people and pets. But a consistent art practice can be part of your day that you can look forward to, and where the rest of the world melts away (if only for a little while).

Whether you are an artist wanting to improve (or experiment with) a new technique or you simply want a way to unwind after a long day, just getting started can be a big challenge. You might have the idea or the hope to do so, but how do you begin? This is why I love daily projects. By laying some ground "rules" and coming up with some guidelines, you give yourself a place to start and come back to each day. And by setting aside the time to work on it, you are honoring yourself and your time.

In this section, I speak with four different artists about their own foray into daily (or near daily) projects that had a significant impact on their lives and work. Amy Reader, Steph Evans, Amy Jones, and Hannah Claire Somerville have dedicated a significant amount of time to them. For some, like Steph and Hannah, the projects are still ongoing. The two Amys each share how the short sprints jump-started new bodies of work. In speaking with each of them, the work was about more than the routine. It was about what that practice illuminates when we're taking the time to look.

Daily projects, no matter their duration, are personal. They are also challenging because the amount of time you'll work on them is often stipulated. But trust me, you can do it. Each artist has their way of relating to a project and making it work for them, just as you do. Allow their stories and tips to be your guide. The uniting thread throughout each is to give yourself grace as you work on a project.

In the first two chapters of the book, you've created work that's based on objects—whether that's an object of treasure or repair. This part will empower you to start and finish your own weeklong project. I'll go over how you can begin to figure out what that will look like, and some psychology-backed tips that will help set you up for success.

Finishing a daily project is deeply satisfying and empowering. Once you complete it, chances are that you'll want to do it again (and again).

Amy Reader

If planning is a superpower, artist Amy Reader has it. She understands the potential—and freedom—that comes from starting and finishing a daily project, and how a simple plan can help make success happen.

Amy had always been an artistic kid and was drawn to making things as a way to relax. "I learned to sew when I was six years old by watching VHS tapes," she tells me from her studio in Portland, Oregon. "I fell in love with textiles. Both of my grandmothers are and were textile people. One of my grandmothers knits and crochets, prolifically, and my other grandmother was a quilter."

Amy took her creativity to college and majored in art. But despite her rich background and passion for fiber art, Amy was primarily drawing and painting. Something, however, just wasn't right. Her work wasn't coming together in a way she was happy with. And then one day, she had an "Aha!" moment.

"I had been trying to get texture and dimension in my two-dimensional work," Amy recalls. "I was obsessing over details and trying all sorts of weird things." Then, it dawned to her: she could use fabric! How had she never thought of it before? "I can build up texture and dimension with felt and textiles in a way that I'm not getting with paint, in a way that I'm not getting with all these other materials."

The artistic revelation set her on a path that she's still on today, and it's one that has benefited from working on daily projects. She started her first 100-day project, in which she'd work on the artistic endeavor every day for about three months, during a time when she had a creatively (and physically) demanding job as a window display coordinator.

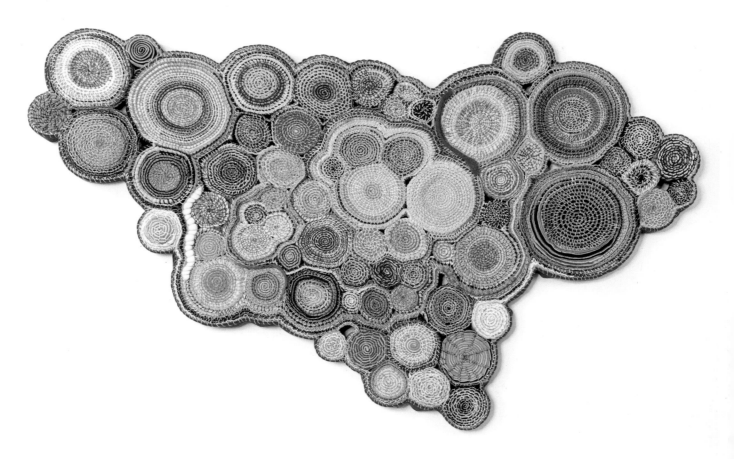

By the time Amy got home from work, she was exhausted. But not wanting to turn over all of her creative energy to someone else, she aimed to start and finish a watercolor-painting project. Amy accomplished it by waking up 30 minutes earlier each day and creating her art before work. (For "not a morning person," this was a big deal.)

Once you've completed one of these every-single-day endeavors, it's easy to want to have that feeling of accomplishment over and over again. That's how Amy felt. "This is the coolest thing I've ever done," she smiles when recalling it. "I'm going to do it forever." She didn't do the 100-day project forever, but over the next three years she did complete two and half of them and enjoyed it every time.

The watercolor paintings were her first 100-day project, and Amy sought to start a new one the following year, in 2019. At that point, she was at a different stage in her life. No longer making window displays, she was now working for herself and making a lot of jewelry. "I hadn't had a

Then, it dawned to her: she could use fabric! How had she never thought of it before?

reason to really push myself to do something large," she explains. "I hadn't made any large-scale fiber work since college, when it was kind of my job to do big work that was impressive for [exhibitions] and things like that."

Amy saw the 100-day project as a way to break out of the repetition she felt when making jewelry. She approached the new endeavor with a plan—sort of. She didn't call it a plan, but rather some stipulations that helped the project take an amorphous shape.

The guidelines that Amy gave herself related to logistics over the content of the piece. "I told myself I was going to sew for at least 30 minutes a day. There was no other goal besides sewing and making my largest work yet." Amy's goal was to make something that measured bigger than 3½ feet.

"It just needed to be something that I cared about," Amy says, "that I wanted to push myself on." She would start by exploring a fiber art technique she began in 2015. Back then, however, she didn't have a name for her approach of taking coils of wool and stitching the strips together to create a form that resembles the center of a geode split in two.

Years after Amy began creating her coiled wool, she discovered that what she was doing did, in fact, have a name. "It falls under the category of a technique that is named standing wool, [which is] a rug-making technique that fell out of use after the Industrial Revolution," she explains. "It was used to make thrifty rag rugs. But it was slow. It couldn't be mechanized."

Although it was not widely used, Amy eventually got in contact with another contemporary artist using the same approach. From there, she was able to learn about its history and understand how her work is different. "I consider myself under the umbrella," she explains, "but I [don't use] classic standing-wool techniques." Standing wool has to be constructed for durability. Amy sews on top of the coils—you can see the stitches in her work—which is a big construction liability were it to be a rug. "Your feet are gonna tear those stitches out; and I [also] put beads and needle felt on top." More beautiful liability.

One thing to account for, especially during an extended daily project, is just how you are going to complete it

when life takes you outside your home or studio. If that happens, can you bring your work with you? Will you be able to keep it up? Amy had to contend with this while working on her coils. She traveled to Scotland with her husband while he was on a choir tour. The wool went with her. She sewed on bus rides, much to the curiosity of other passengers. "I schlepped my textiles all over Scotland," she shares, "[and] it was quite the conversation point."

Amy named the finished piece *Kaleidoscope* because it ended up encompassing a variety of ideas, concepts, textiles, and "all sorts of weird things." Together, those things pushed her work forward in ways she didn't anticipate. Before the project began, she built a formula for the small jewelry pieces she had been producing. But expanding her scale via the 100-day project and having the freedom to follow her whims made a formula impossible.

"I said, 'Whatever happens is what happens.' The goal is to make something really big and learn about your work." Not only from an aesthetic perspective, but the "why" in her work.

"Something that has been really important for my process," Amy explains, "is I think about the stitches that I make as a conversation—and a record of a conversation with my work." Every stitch is a mark of time (the seconds it takes to make a stitch), and as she works, there is a physical record of the time spent on it.

"Record keeping is something that I've always had a bit of an obsession with, like recording all my time and recording my days. Part of my process—and something that was really integral to choosing the 100-day project the way that I did—is that I love thinking about my work as this record of time and a record of a conversation that I had with a work that only I can interpret."

But that conversation goes both ways. We can interpret what Amy is saying through our lens, and bring our references and experiences when viewing her work.

Bringing yourself to a work is best done when you have time to study its characteristics. Amy's 100-day project allowed her to experiment with the *Kaleidoscope* surface design. "I did the couching stitch to bind roving and yarn into the stitches as I went," she says as an example, "and that led me to ultimately adding in beads and sequins and

"I said, 'Whatever happens is what happens.' The goal is to make something really big and learn about your work."

other similar textural materials on top of my work where I allow there to be more dimension than just the stitches." Amy doesn't think that she would have gone that far in that direction with her work had she not dedicated the time to do so.

With seemingly endless roads to travel, the project never became tedious. Even on the days when she was feeling tired or frustrated, she honored her commitment to her coils. It turned out that the starting was the hardest part; a half hour would fly by and easily become an hour.

The ritual of carving out time for making continues long past the end of *Kaleidoscope*. She blocks out at least two hours of her working days for sewing and protects the time by not allowing herself to take on additional tasks. When she's focused just on sewing, she has the time and space to figure out where her work is going next.

The beauty of a 100-day project is that it is long enough for you to explore a subject or technique or have the freedom to create within a prescribed amount of time. But be sure to consider when you have what you needed out of a project, and be open to changing directions.

Amy began a third iteration of a 100-day project the year after *Kaleidoscope* but didn't finish it. She landed on a couple of ideas that she was excited about, and shifted gears to explore those instead. Success no longer meant doing 100 days of something, as it had the first two times. The structure wasn't serving her any longer, and she reframed success as the project leading her to the next great idea.

Even without maintaining (or continuing) the daily practice aspect that most recent time, she says, "I didn't have the same body of work or the same large piece to look back on afterward, [but] I had ideas that have been really valuable and meaningful and exciting for me, because of the time that I gave to the project."

Steph Evans

Steph Evans was pregnant with her first daughter and living with the stress of running her own recruiting business. It wasn't the type of pressure that comes with a major life event; this was the something-has-to-change kind of stress. After giving birth to her child five and a half weeks early, she had an "awakening." Steph gave up the business and decided that she needed

She found that the lack of sleep from being a new mom made it seemingly impossible to retain memories.

to do something that would force her to slow down. Crafting was it.

She started with cross-stitch but found the limitations of the designs and the grid system too restrictive. Freehand embroidery, she discovered, offered her a way to stitch whatever she wanted without the same conventions of cross-stitch. With that freedom, she drew a "load of boobs." "I did a boobie doodle," she tells me from her home in Manchester, UK, "because I was going down the route of wanting to do something related to body positivity after having a baby."

Other people were interested in her boobie doodles, and Steph used it as an opportunity to create her first embroidery kit. She continued to experiment with her work, and it was the discovery of thread journaling that marked a turning point for her, not only in her artistic practice and business but in how she moved through the world.

Steph started her first thread journal in 2019, determined to create a new illustration of her day every day. She found it beneficial, but ultimately the task became a chore. "It felt like a to-do instead of a ta-da," she explains, conveying that thread journaling should feel like a revelation, a gift we give to ourselves, rather than a chore.

"I realized forcing you to do a stitch a day takes a bit of the joy out of it. It makes it quite high pressure. And I want people to really enjoy the moment, because with embroidery, you can't rush it. You've got to slow down, and it's like an active meditation."

Mindful making is just one of the benefits that Steph has discovered during her years of thread journaling. The hoop acts as an unconventional memory album and is a place to permanently record her everyday life. This was particularly important to Steph, since she found that the lack of sleep from being a new mom made it seemingly impossible to retain memories—even with so many wonderful things happening around her.

Having a stitched record was a motivating factor to begin journaling, and it helped. "I would say I probably remember 90 percent [of what the icons represent] or maybe even more," she shares, "because while you're creating the miniature stitch, you are thinking about that moment. So you've reflected on that moment, while you're just con-

centrating on what you're creating."

Not everything included in her thread journal is a happy memory. Authenticity is important to Steph. For things that are too painful to stitch because they feel fresh—like when her dog died—she is careful to give herself that space and time to properly mourn the loss before working on an illustration about it.

Although keeping a stitched journal can be an emotionally painful experience, it is a display and reminder of our resilience in the face of difficulties. Collectively, we don't have to look back far in time to see this in action. The year 2020 was hard for everyone, Steph and her family included.

It was during this time that she found out she was pregnant with her second daughter. Naturally, she recorded it in her thread journal. Steph stitched two tiny little lines (indicating a positive pregnancy test) on the day she found out, and also recorded the various scans she had throughout her pregnancy. They were made challenging because she had to go to them by herself; due to COVID precautions, her partner wasn't allowed to attend.

But looking at the hoop from that year, Steph sees magical moments from that time she wouldn't have remembered otherwise. "There are loads of little starlings; there were just hundreds of them wandering in the garden," she says, looking at the hoop. "We were all amazed at these birds that had landed in the garden." She doesn't think she would've remembered it otherwise. "There are a lot of things on here that potentially would have just been deleted out of my memory during the year of COVID."

The hoop's existence offers more gentle reminders, too: that we can persist in the face of great difficulties, and that life is rarely all good or all bad. There is always a crack of light in the dark.

As the thread journaling extends a line now through the years, Steph has made logistical changes to how she works on it. She no longer requires herself to stitch every day, and she can catch up on days when she has time. To aid in memory making, she takes pictures or videos each day of the things she'd like to stitch. These are things that catch her eye, such as a rainbow or a pretty leaf, that feel meaningful and make for an aesthetically pleasing icon in the hoop.

But even that is up for negotiation. "I would sometimes prefer to spend time developing a really detailed miniature memory, rather than just little things from different days," Steph explains. Giving into that urge is a strategy for when life gets in the way.

"If I've been really busy, and I've not been able to do it as much as I'd like to, I can cherry-pick the key moments I really want to record. And that tends to get me in the mood again." She'll then go back and add embroideries for the days she missed.

Just as there's no right way to write in a journal, you can decide how memory stitching will fit into your life. Perhaps it makes sense to stitch a little something every day, or you can commit only to the weekend, or you may want to save it for the times you travel.

Steph formats her thread journal in a way that's standard for a yearlong project in an embroidery hoop. She starts by stitching the year into the middle of the composition, and in recent years has put some decoration around it. Of course, that convention is not the only way to do it, and Steph works with people to help develop their thread journals. Some people, for instance, will embroider a word in place of the year that they intend to focus on for the following 365 days. A meaningful symbol in the middle is also another option, such as a sun for happiness or a flower for growth.

Because thread journaling is chronicling time, moving clockwise around the hoop is a natural choice. Doing so helps Steph keep track of the year, even without explicitly dividing it by the month. Although tracking a clock might seem obvious, it might not make sense, depending on the format. "There are ones that people have done with their surname [in the middle] and then split it into four, because there were four members of a family," she said. "They had each of the people's names around the outside. So when things happened related to those people, they could put it in their section."

Aside from stitching the name of the year, Steph refrains from using words to describe a day. "I try to do pictures more than words," she says, "because [just putting words in] can be very easy to slip into. I think you lose the

meaning a little bit." She does, however, make an exception. "When a child's born, I usually put their name on. It's really helpful for me to remember birthdays."

Planning and stipulations aside, the business of actually making the stitches happen is typically done completely freehand. Rarely does Steph draw on the fabric for a design, the exceptions being something such as sunglasses, which are very symmetrical and easier to get right with a little sketching. For those moments, she uses a heat-erasable fabric pen because you can blast it with a hairdryer on hot heat and remove the ink.

"For the vast majority," Steph muses, "I'd say I freehand stitch it because I find that a lot of the time, you'll just use one individual strand of floss (out of the six) to get that detail. So I can look at it as drawing with thread rather than embroidery." Most of the images are simple, especially on such a small scale, so the back stitch is an easy technique to use.

Thread journaling chronicles life, and it reflects both memories and the intangible lessons that come with living, from highlighting the good times to reminding us of our ability to be resilient. And there's another unseen aspect that appears only when you're in the thick of stitching: letting it go. Let go of expectations and let go of the frustration of making something that you don't like. It is tempting to cut out a design that you think looks bad, but Steph implores you to leave it.

"I always say to people, even if you completely mess something up, leave it, do not unpick it," she says. "By the end of the project, if you're doing it in the same way that I do by going in a clockwise motion, your very first stitch will be right next to your last stitch. And you'll be able to visually see how much you've progressed over that period, whether it be a year, three months, or 10 years . . . you will see how far you've come."

"I always say to people, even if you completely mess something up, leave it, do not unpick it."

Amy Jones

It was early 2020, and like the rest of us, Amy Jones was confronted with a new reality of COVID lockdowns. In New Zealand, where she was living, the country placed restrictions on its residents a lot later than in other places around the world, so Amy had an idea of what was coming. It was scary, especially for Amy; she has a rare chronic illness called achalasia.

Beyond the health concerns were her family—namely, her (lovingly described) "clingy" children. With the unprecedented and uncertain times, Amy turned to a daily embroidery project as a grounding force for her at the start of the pandemic.

Amy, who works under the name Cheese Before Bedtime, began the project she calls the COVID diaries. "With the kids home during four weeks of lockdown in April 2020

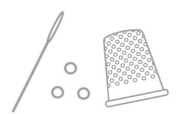

and feeling a bit claustrophobic," she tells me over email, "I found myself unmotivated and uninspired. So easily I could have focused on the kids' homework (and keeping sane!), but I love embroidery so much and thought I had better keep my hands moving, even if only a little bit each day." A daily project would help keep her accountable, so she decided to illustrate her day each day and share it with her fans on social media.

The project reflected her days—a "lockdown diary"—and the emphasis was on the content over style. "I committed to illustrating and stitching a little outline of an idea, feeling, or happening from that day onto a large piece of fabric," she explains.

Aesthetically, it was a departure from her previous work. It was the first time she had grouped small illustrations using a single thread hue. "Normally I would've added in colors or textures, but this was just simple black outlines and detailed images," Amy continues. "There's normally a lot of planning involved with my projects and themes to create a range of work. It was nice to be a bit looser in my planning and stitch what I felt daily. It was fun to not know the outcome."

Although Amy abbreviated her process for the sake of simplicity, hand embroidery still takes awhile. During the month of strict lockdown, she worked between one and three hours on each of her illustrations. None of her designs were preplanned, since she wanted the overall piece to feel authentic even though it was an unconventional format for a diary to take. But Amy did strive for visual variety in the designs and included a couple of people, some animals, and a quote or two. This was another small way to creatively challenge herself while still honoring the deeply personal nature of the project.

Amy sketches all of her designs beforehand, and she maintained the practice throughout her coronavirus diaries. During the daytime, she drew the design on paper and created the outline for it by using black ink before tracing it onto fabric, using a light box. Nighttime brought Netflix and stitching to complete the day's design. Occasionally, she would embroider multiple autobiographical elements in a day in order to fill unexpected space in the overall design.

"It was nice to be a bit looser in my planning and stitch what I felt daily. It was fun to not know the outcome."

"I was actually surprised to have
followers mention how they looked
forward to my daily posts, how important
it was to them too."

Of all her illustrations included in the project, Amy has several that she looks back on with fondness. "There were many themes in my daily stitchings," she says, "but the ones I liked the most were the whimsy and the humor."

Her bra image is one standout. "It's undone and off! I only realized really late on in the month that no one would come knocking at the door and I wasn't going anywhere, so I could take the bra off! [It was] so freeing." And like many, Amy was reminded of the importance of her home. "I also loved the stitching of our home exterior. It really is my sanctuary and kept us well housed during that time. It was a safe space."

Like Steph and her stitch diaries, Amy chose to include some meaningful text. "I love the haiku from my granddad that he made using a play on my names Amy Rose. It was Amy Rose / Sat on a Tack / Amy rose."

Whimsy and humor proved an important part of her piece. Not only were these bits fun to think of and to stitch, but they were a source of much-needed distraction. "This [diary] kept me going when I was anxious about rising cases and fear of catching COVID. The daily press conferences and news articles were relentless and all consuming, but the humor of the work helped me get through and others enjoyed it too."

Knowing that others were awaiting her diary entries kept Amy powering through the days when she just didn't feel like stitching. "Sharing my work on Instagram kept me connected with others," she recalls, "and I enjoyed hearing from my followers who could relate to the different items each day." Being vulnerable (and even funny) can feel nerve racking; what will people think? Am I oversharing? Amy's project proved that people were looking for connection, especially during the spring of 2020.

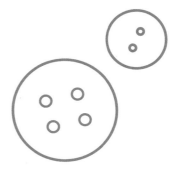

"I was actually surprised to have followers mention how they looked forward to my daily posts, how important it was to them too. It was nice to engage in this different raw way that wasn't overly edited."

Having some sort of accountability—whether that is to an audience on social media or just your best friend—is one thing that helped make Amy's COVID project a success. She also recommends beginning a project when the inspiration iron is hot and you have a feeling of excite-

ment pulsing through you. Doing so will build momentum and buoy you on the doldrum days. Timing is also important. "Try to carve out your most-productive hours for it. Listen to podcasts or music, or watch a show while doing it so that time flies," she suggests.

Committing to this project showed her new meaning of progress. "I learned that small actions every day can create something beautiful and intriguing," Amy shares, looking back on her stitched diary. "I had the finished piece in my bedroom and could stare at it for ages, looking at all the little details and remembering those days. I'm a terrible photo taker, and my memory is not the best, but these little images take me back and make me smile."

Amy sells much of her work through her shop, but she could never part with her COVID-era diaries. They are full of special memories and represent the power of creativity in scary and uncertain times.

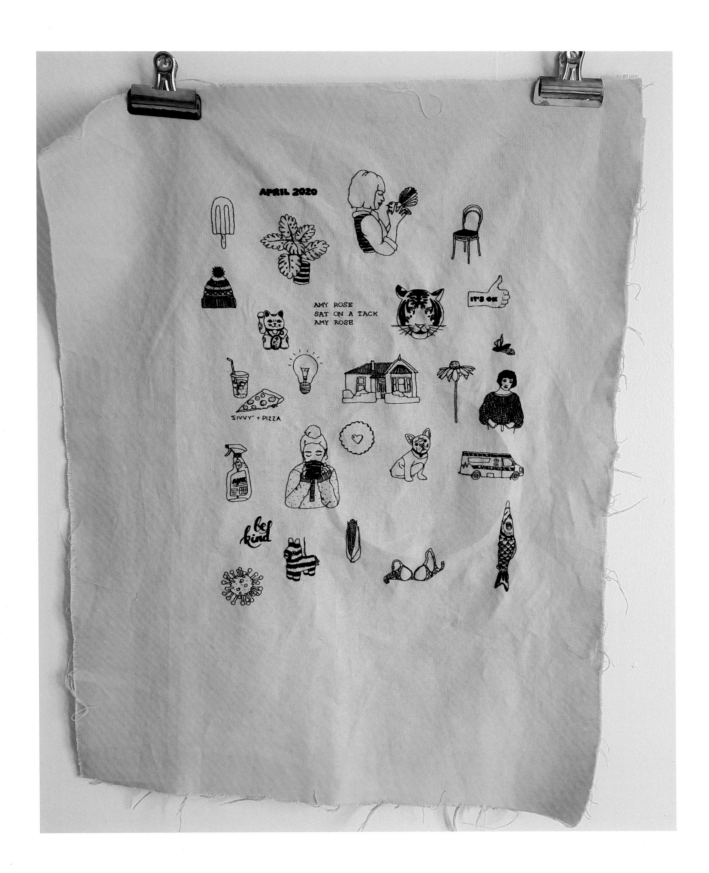

Hannah Claire Somerville

We mark the days in different ways. Some tick the checkboxes on our to-do lists, while others, like Hannah Claire Somerville, have made a stitch a day (at least) for the better part of seven years.

In 2016, she came up with the idea of the 1 Year of Stitches project. Like the 100-day project, the length of time is in the name, and it exists under a set of loose guidelines that allow you to make the embroidery project your own. And to help make it successful, there is accountability baked into the parameters.

The guidelines are as follows: make at least a stitch every day (if that's not possible, at least take a photo of your

"What if I captured a physical representation of my daily commute? What would that pattern look like?"

Hannah Claire Somerville's completed projects in 2016 (*left*) and 2017 (*right*)

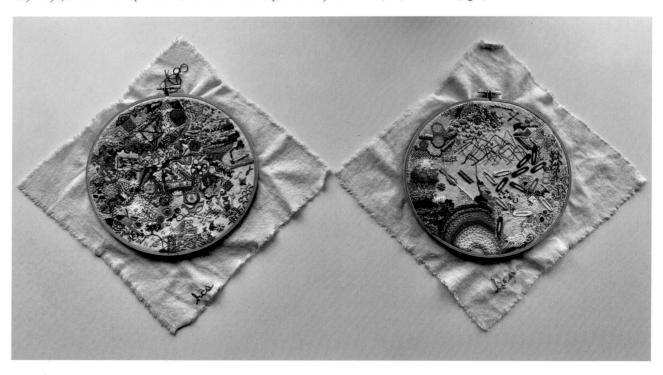

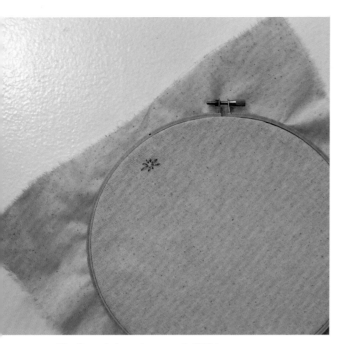

The first stitch on January 1, 2016

Detail from May 21, 2016, in which she removed some threads because she was unhappy with what she had done

project that day), take a picture that shows your project, date your picture and write a few words about the embroidery or your day, and share online with the hashtag #1yearofstitches.

There's another private stipulation that Hannah Claire Somerville added to the project for herself. "The number one was," she tells me from her home in the Bay Area, "I had to be kind to myself." Hannah Claire Somerville had a formal art education where the critiques could be brutal. "I was at a point in my life where I didn't want to be really hard on myself because that takes the joy out of it."

The prolific painter Wayne Thiebaud also inspired a softer view of the expectations that Hannah Claire Somerville could place on herself. "He always talked about the joy of making and the joy of painting," she explains, "and I always thought that that's the kind of artist I want to be. I know there is the trope of a dark and artsy person, but I do it for joy."

Hannah Claire Somerville has long been interested in daily routines, from a practical standpoint—the more you do something, the easier it comes to you—as well as a spiritual sense. The 1 Year of Stitches project came to her like a stroke of inspiration. She was on a bus, commuting from her home in Oakland to San Francisco for her graduate program in museum studies.

"I was excited about the program," she recalls. "I was also nervous because I was wondering [if] I was getting away from art." The program was creative but much more studious than she had anticipated. This all got her thinking. What would her daily commute *look* like? "You're doing this repetition every day," Hannah Claire Somerville says, "and that got me to think about, well, what if I captured a physical representation of my daily commute? What would that pattern look like?"

The 2016 project ended up being a complement to her life at the time, which involved a lot of reading, writing, and internships at museums. She would work on her stitches in the evening, but if she had time while she was commuting, she'd do it then too.

Hannah Claire Somerville's daily contributions were small—it required only one stitch a day, after all—and she was able to share her process with others. It's something many artists refrain from sharing online. But she wanted to show how artwork gets made, and that success, as well as failure, is all part of the journey.

With the loose guidelines and emphasis on grace and kindness toward herself, the beginning of 1 Year of Stitches was trying anything and seeing what stuck.

"At first, I was going with whatever color and sometimes would be inspired by if I saw, [for instance], an orange persimmon against a blue sky on a tree when I was walking. 'Oh, I'll use orange and orange and blue today.'"

As time went on, she experimented with the format by assigning a color to each month. This challenged her to differentiate the design so that it didn't become an amorphous blob of one hue. "That was when I [began] exploring different embroidery techniques," Hannah Claire Somerville recalls. "I think that was an unexpected part of this project that I really enjoyed: the opportunity to expand my repertoire of stitches, and to really hone that skill a little bit more."

Finishing any sort of daily project is a rewarding experience. It's proof that you can commit to a goal and see it through. But with each passing year, the finishing might seem less important because you've been able to conquer it before. Hannah Claire Somerville had a few successful years of completing the project she designed. A quick scroll through her @1yearofstitches Instagram will show that she's paused the project.

"I'm never mad at myself for it," she says. It's understanding that there are other forces at play, and some iterations of the project don't lend themselves to a whole year. "In 2020," Hannah Claire Somerville explains, "I did it very differently. Instead of doing more of the mark making and patternmaking, [it] was specific to where everyone was feeling boxed in, and I did it as a pandemic response." This was before most of us realized that we weren't going to flatten the coronavirus curve in just a few weeks. "What I realized was, 'Okay, I don't think this pandemic is ending anytime soon. When does this project end as a daily practice?'"

Hannah Claire Somerville had every intention of completing 1 Year of Stitches in 2022, before she stopped in February. "I was like, wait, I'm six months postpartum.

"That was an unexpected part of this project that I really enjoyed: the opportunity to expand my repertoire of stitches."

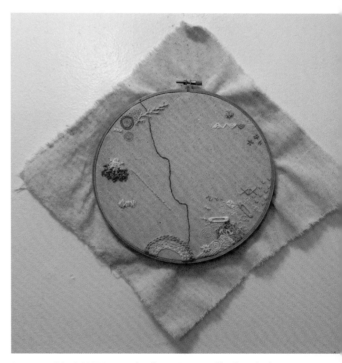

January 20, 2017. Hannah Claire Somerville decided to stick to one color family a month.

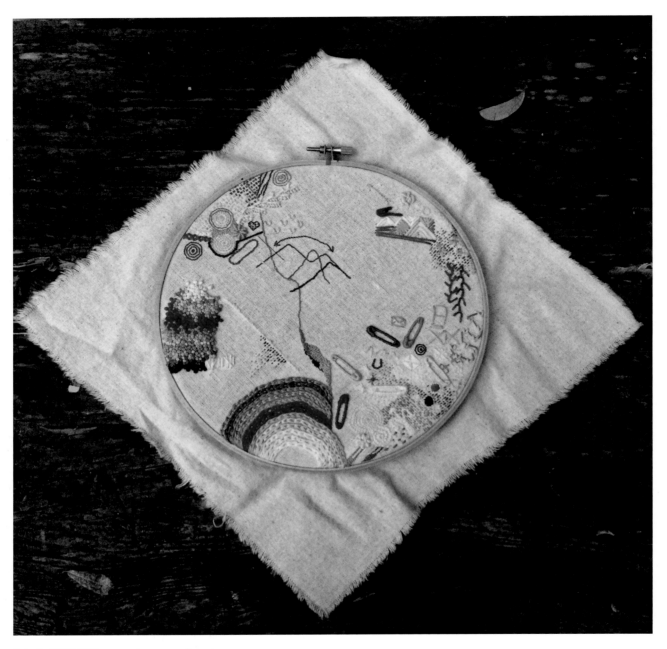

July 3, 2017. "This was taken at my favorite camp-
ground in Northern California, which sadly the road
to get to it was washed away in a storm in the winter of
2017/2018 so I haven't been able to go back," Hannah
Claire Somerville says. "I'm really happy I have the
memory of embroidering there."

What am I thinking?" The fits and starts illustrate how life moves forward and how these yearlong endeavors follow us through the ups and downs.

"Something I hoped that I could share with other artists who picked up this project, or people who had never stitched before and wanted to try it, was to make it accessible and fun," she says. "So if there were those days that I didn't [stitch], I just was like, 'Okay, I just didn't today, and I still took a photo and I still talked about why.'"

It could've been that Hannah Claire Somerville was doing something fun, or she was deeply engaged in life that day. But regardless of whether she put needle to fabric, the long endeavor has been a constant throughout the last many years of her life. The project has followed her from being engaged to being married to having children. Through 1 Year of Stitches, the practice has offered an unconventional reminder to be present with the people she cares about in her life.

The open-ended nature of the project makes it something for everyone, and we can all take what we want from it. Hannah Claire Somerville recommends diving in—don't be afraid to start with whatever fabric, size of hoop, or time of day you have right now.

"What I love about this is that this is not math. There's no wrong answer."

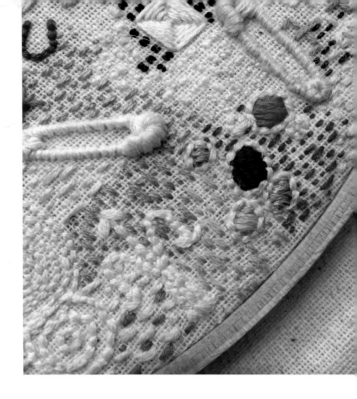

August 21, 2017 (detail). 1 Year of Stitches inspired new projects. "I started embroidering safety pins as at the time wearing a safety pin was a sign of solidarity with vulnerable groups including minorities, immigrants, women and members of the L.G.B.T.Q. community as sadly abuse was on the rise," she explains. "It sparked a series of pieces about this."

Detail of August 8, 2018

Start and Finish a Weeklong Project

Having a project that you return to each day can be a
grounding experience. It can also feel like a burden.
I'm familiar with both. In 2017, I began Hannah Claire
Somerville's 1 Year of Stitches project, in which I stitched on
the same hoop every day from January 1 to December 31.

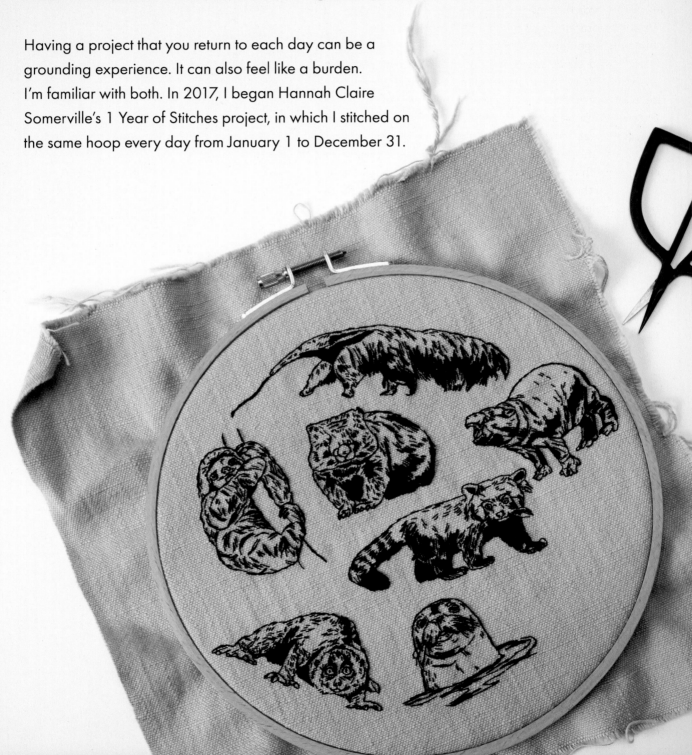

It was challenging to make sure that I embroidered every day—making sure I documented it too—even when I was on vacation or struggling to maintain other responsibilities in my life. But I look back on the project as an integral part of my embroidery journey. I used the project as a way to learn and practice new stitches, and it helped me connect with the larger embroidery community.

I've tried twice more, in 2019 and 2021, to complete another 1 Year of Stitches project. Both times I stopped before the year was up. I attribute my "failure" in 2019 to moving halfway across the country. I think I made it to May, and that's being generous with my memory. In 2021, I was too ambitious with my plans and burned out by the end of March that year.

As the other artists in this section have shared, I too refused to let myself feel bad about not completing these daily projects in 2019 and 2021. Think about all the things you want to do—and enjoy doing—and then think about all the things that can happen over a year. There is plenty that can knock you off track. But that doesn't mean you can't benefit from trying a daily project. I jumped into the deep end with 1 Year of Stitches, but planning a weeklong project is a great way to ignite your creativity and build habits that will help you treasure every day through art.

Planning and Brainstorming

To start any big project, consider journaling. I find that it helps explore my feelings, particularly if I give myself an open-ended topic and write about it. I can say whatever I want—no restrictions. The words and sentiments that bubble up in the journaling tell me what's important to me, what I'm worried about, and what I hope will go well. I recommend grabbing a journal and doing some light writing about the next ideas. If you don't want to write, it's helpful to mentally reflect on them.

Start with Your Why

Start with your "why." Consider: Why are you attempting this project in the first place? Is there a particular aspect of it that interests you? What do you hope to learn by doing a project like this? There can be many reasons that you want to work on a daily project. Maybe you want to

Daily projects are a way of saying that for a while each day, for a set number of days, I am going make my creative time a priority.

jump-start a series of artwork you've dreamed of working on. Perhaps you're going to use it as a way to connect with others. You might want to challenge yourself to see if you're capable of it. All are valid reasons to embark on it.

Daily projects, above all, allow us to reclaim some time for ourselves. They are a way of saying that for a while each day, for a set number of days, I am going make my creative time a priority.

Explore What Interests You

Once you have your "why" nailed down, it's time to figure out what interests you. A daily project, with its measured intensity, is a great way to explore a topic that tugs at you. You likely have something—or many things—in mind. If not, here are some places to start.

Pick a subject that you love. It's easy to forget that you will be spending time on this project each day, so select a subject that naturally interests you. This will make it easier to work on during the days that you're just not feeling it.

Use it as a form of reflection. Use fabric as a place to journal and reflect on your day. Like Steph, you can incorporate something from your day into the piece to look back on later.

Go granular on what you're already doing. Expand on an aspect of your current body of artwork. Use the project as a way to explore the nitty-gritty of a technique. Alternatively, use it to go big and work on something you've always wanted to try but never had time for.

This is how I approached my daily project in 2021. I embroider a lot of custom pet portraits, from sweet kitties to silly dogs, but they were mostly on a smaller scale. I used my daily project as a way to work on one portrait each month. In doing so, I played with color and embroidered a level of detail that I hadn't had the opportunity to incorporate in my custom portraits before.

Dive into something new. Use your daily project as a way to experiment or learn new approaches. One example is learning new embroidery stitches. You could create a design in which you'll try a new type of stitch each day. By the end of the project, you will be comfortable with the techniques and can incorporate them into other projects.

Making Creativity a Habit

Planning is an essential part of tackling a daily project. As I've learned firsthand, you can have an idea you really love, but if you don't have a solid system for how you intend to execute it, you're already trying to push a boulder uphill.

Human behavior favors low resistance; things are easier to accomplish when distractions are out of the way. Long-distance runners will sleep in their running clothes just so they have no choice but to go for a jog as soon as they wake up. You don't need to sleep next your embroidery, but having it alongside your coffee maker helps ensure you'll work on it first thing in the morning.

Once you've settled on an idea for your project, envision how you will make it happen. Shift from thinking about the goal of your endeavor—what you want to learn or how you want it to look—and think about creating a system, an environment, where that will happen. You could, like Amy Reader did, wake up a little earlier each day. Your project is already laid out for you, so it's simple to begin. Or, like Amy Jones, you like to spend your evenings watching Netflix. Use this as an opportunity to embroider while you binge-watch.

Timing Helps

If you find your project impossible to repeat at that certain time of day, that's a sign that you should reconsider when you work on it. The people who appear self-disciplined aren't more so than the rest of us; they have just oriented their lives to make the right choices easier to make. The spirit might be willing, but if something is too difficult to access or to fit into your schedule, it will be much harder to accomplish it—no matter how determined you are.

You can begin your project on any day you like. But if possible, be strategic about it. Timing can help you better achieve your goals with the project and see it to completion.

There's a reason that we make new year's resolutions. Psychologists Jason Riis, Hengchen Dai, and Katy Milkman explain the phenomenon in a chapter titled "The Fresh-Start Effect: Motivational Boosts beyond New Year's Resolutions."[1] While it's possible we can accomplish big goals within the span of a year, most of us don't do that. We act based on our habits or impulses, not our goals.

Mistakes count as progress because they help us eliminate what we don't want to be doing.

The hyena patch that inspired my daily project

"And yet," the authors write, "there are some moments when we are a little more willing and able to rise to our goals. In those moments, we feel the need to step up, do better, and become our ideal self." They refer to them as "fresh starts."

Timing your project to these "fresh starts" could be as simple as choosing to start at the beginning of the week. Starting your stitches on Monday rather than Thursday. This wraps it up on Sunday (if you're doing a weeklong project). But for projects that are longer than a week, such as a month, three months, or even a year, consider tying them to the beginning of the month, the beginning of a season, or the first day of January. Doing so allows you to say to yourself, "This month . . ." or "This fall . . ." or "This year . . ." It has power.

Working on Your Daily Project

Once you have an idea and a plan, grab the supplies you'll need and get started on the day of your choosing. Maybe you spent a lot of time considering the concept and logistics behind your project. Let that go once you begin making the work.

The biggest benefit of having this dedicated project is time. Spread out over days, weeks, and months, there are a lot of opportunities to experiment and to see where your mind and materials will take you. Be open to your whims. Follow them. At best, you will discover a new path on your journey of making. If that doesn't work out, however, you'll have tried something and can learn from it. There's even the possibility that it can inform other elements of your work. Mistakes count as progress because they help us eliminate what we don't want to be doing.

Enjoy the time you spend each day by practicing elements of mindfulness. Try, as much as possible, to be in the moment. This is as hard and as easy as it sounds. It's easy for our minds to wander while we work. But in whatever way you choose to work, whether it's on the couch while watching TV, listening to music, or sitting in silence, focus on what is happening in the present. Listen to the words the podcast host is saying. Feel the needle in your hand. Notice how the thread lays across the fabric.

There is so much that we can miss when we let the past

and future dictate the here and now. Past reflection and future planning are vital, of course, but it's a gift you can give yourself when you focus on present-moment awareness.

As the artists in this section have shown, there are many ways to approach a daily project and practice. For another perspective, here is how I approached my week-long project.

I start with my "why." What do I want to accomplish with this project? This is the easy part for me, since it's something I've wanted to explore for a while: embroidering wild animals. I currently work on a lot of custom pet portraits for people who want to celebrate their favorite cat, dog, bunny, blue-tongued skink—you name it. But I haven't had much of a chance to draw animals outside of domesticated pets. That was until I was commissioned to create a patch for someone who loves hyenas.

The hyena was a great opportunity to work on an animal that I had never tried drawing before, and sketching its snout and mouselike ears made me want to draw other wide creatures. But with the obligations of everyday life, that proved challenging. I knew that if I want to explore this idea in a meaningful way, a daily project would be the way to do it.

Before beginning, I decided to spend up to a few hours a day on this project. That time would go fast, so I needed to plan accordingly. My work is typically in full color; I use anywhere between 10 and 20 DMC floss hues in a portrait. The time constraints offered another way in which I could experiment with my style. For my daily animal project, I worked only in black thread (similar to Amy Jones) and created outlines of the creature portrait along with some dramatic shading to give them depth. The embroideries were more than a few inches tall, so I needed to figure out what details are important to include and exclude.

With the stipulations in mind, it was time to decide where and how the project would take form. I selected one piece of linen-blend fabric to work on, and I drew the animals on my iPad each day and printed them on stick-

Feel the needle in your hand. Notice how the thread lays across the fabric.

and-stitch stabilizer. When I was done with the weeklong project, I soaked the stabilizer in warm water to remove it. At that point, my project was finished.

I'm a morning person, and I love to embroider after I wake up and before my daily meditation. It was during this time that I stitched my embroidery and also drew the animal I was going to work on the following day.

I decided to start embroidering my project on Monday, and the final day was Sunday. But because I am stitching on stabilizer, I wanted to have it printed and ready to go when Monday morning arrived. It required that I did a little work the Sunday before. It was an extra step I don't mind taking, because when Monday morning arrives, I hit the ground stitching.

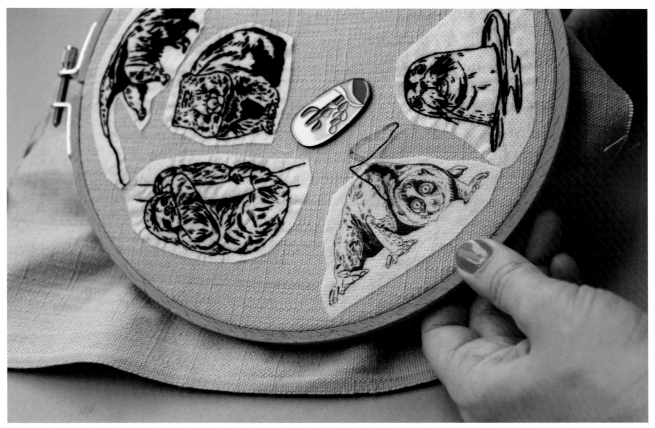

By working on the wild-animal portraits in this way, I'm hopeful that it will lead to new possibilities for my commissioned pet portraits. Much like Amy Reader's 100-day project informed her overall body of work, I see this project as a springboard for my future pieces.

Remember, daily projects are a marathon and not a sprint. To succeed in completing your project, here are some things to keep in mind.

- Make your practice sustainable by deciding on when and how long you will work on it each day.

- Not every day promises to be amazing, but every day you will make progress on it and learn a little bit more about yourself and your creative process.

- As you work, think about keeping yourself accountable. Whether it's documenting the process each day or just at the start and finish, let others know what you're doing. You're more likely to stick with it, and you'll have people cheering you on—something that we could all use more often.

Whether it's documenting the process each day or just at the start and finish, let others know what you're doing.

PARTING THOUGHTS

There's a lot we can treasure in our lives; we just have to know where to look. With any luck, this book helped you do it (or it will help—Rome wasn't built in a day). My ultimate goal was to empower you in your own creativity with illuminating artist profiles and ways to apply the ideas in each chapter into a physical form.

You don't have to look far to find what you need to be creative. You can tap into it just by being yourself. Each of us has special ways of looking at the world with experiences, thoughts, and perspectives that have shaped us into who we are. Leaning into these intangible elements and giving yourself the time and space to explore them will reveal new treasures, like a diamonds in the rough.

But you might think that your ideas about your own artistic process or image making are set in stone and that there's no room for improvement. I know from my own experience that they are not.

I've been making my own art for many years, and still, in talking with the artists in *Threads of Treasure*, I found many things I'd like to try. I was struck by how many of them experiment with their process, and it made me realize that I don't do that enough in my own practice. I won't replicate that in the same way that they do, but just knowing that is an important reminder for me to let myself play every once in a while.

There's always the opportunity, from this book, to think about how to apply some of these principles to yourself—even if they might seem irrelevant at first. Hannah Claire Somerville touched on that in our conversation when she spoke about how painter Wayne Thiebaud found joy in the act of art making. Her art isn't composed of sweet treats and San Francisco streets like Thiebaud's, but just knowing about his happiness inspired her to do the same.

As much as you can, avoid comparing yourself to any creative. It's cliché, but comparison really is the thief of joy. It's also tempting, but our journeys are our own. There is no standard way of doing things. Another throughline in this book is that every artist found their way, on their own time, and did so in a manner that is unique to them.

But authenticity in art can be hard to come by. Figuring out what lights your fire takes a lot of introspection and years, if not decades, of living in the world and seeing how all the pieces fit together. And then, of course, there is that voice inside your head . . . the one that's not always polite (or right).

It brings to mind something that Hillary Waters Fayle told me during our chat. When she first started embroidery on leaves, her inner critic was loud. "[It was] the self-judgment of 'Oh, that'll never work. That's stupid. You're just trying to do that because of this, or you've seen it before.' Whatever it is."

This mindset can be a virus, infecting anything that you attempt. "It'll stop you in your tracks," Hillary says. "Try to be as free as you can and then quiet that voice, and then lean in toward the things that you really enjoy." When you do that, you can't go wrong. And that's something to treasure.

AFFIRMATIONS FOR CREATIVES

Get into the making mindset with these stitchable cards. Download the patterns at
www.schiffercraft.com/ThreadsOfTreasure.

Every day I find something to treasure.

My creativity has no limits.

I listen to what my creative intuition tells me.

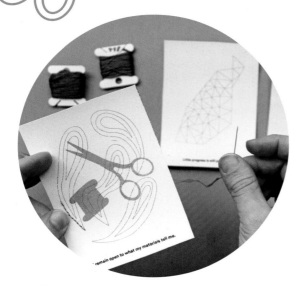

To begin, select a card for the day. Choose a thread color (or colors) and the number of strands you'd like to stitch with. (I used two, but you could use more or fewer.)

Using your needle, poke tiny holes on the lines that you'd like to embroider. You'll determine the space between each hole, but be sure to avoid them being too close together. Then, thread your needle and begin embroidering using your favorite stitches.

Refer to your cards anytime you need a creative boost.

NOTES

Before You Start

1. Alia Crum, "Reframing Your Reality (Part 1)," *Hidden Brain* (podcast), July 18, 2022, produced by Hidden Brain Media, MP3 audio, 48:37, https://hiddenbrain.org/podcast/reframing-your-reality-part-1/.

Displaying Treasures

1. Robin Wall Kimmerer, essay in *Braiding Sweetgrass: Indigenous Wisdom, Scientific Knowledge, and the Teachings of Plants* (Minneapolis: Milkweed, 2020), 183.

Treasuring the Things We Love

1. Owen Mulhern, "The 10 Essential Fast Fashion Statistics," Earth.org. July 28, 2022, https://earth.org/fast-fashion-statistics/.
2. Jake Silbert, "Everyone Hates Shein but No One Wants to Stop Buying It," Highsnobiety, April 13, 2022, https://www.highsnobiety.com/p/shein-valuation-worth-ethical-sustainable/.

Treasuring Everyday Moments

1. Hengchen Dai, Katherine L. Milkman, and Jason Riis, "The Fresh Start Effect: Temporal Landmarks Motivate Aspirational Behavior." *Management Science* 60, no. 10 (June 23, 2014): 10, https://faculty.wharton.upenn.edu/wp-content/uploads/2014/06/Dai_Fresh_Start_2014_Mgmt_Sci.pdf.

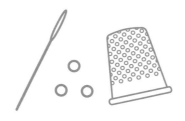

Sara Barnes is an artist and writer who runs the popular blog *Brown Paper Bag* and was previously an editor at My Modern Met. She runs Bear&Bean, an embroidery studio stitching pet portraits and other beloved creatures. Her work has been recognized in *Embroidery*, *American Illustration*, and other publications. She is also the author of *Embroidered Life*. When she's not stitching or writing, she enjoys planning things that bring people together. She is the cofounder of Camp Craftaway, a day camp for crafty adults. She lives in Seattle, Washington.

www.brwnpaperbag.com